Sudden Selector's Guide
to Chemistry Resources

ALCTS/CMS SUDDEN SELECTOR'S SERIES

Sudden Selector's Guide to Business Resources

Sudden Selector's Guide to Communication Studies Resources

Sudden Selector's Guide to Chemistry Resources

ALCTS/CMS SUDDEN SELECTOR'S SERIES, #3

SUDDEN SELECTOR'S GUIDE to Chemistry Resources

ELIZABETH BROWN

Collection Management Section of the Association
for Library Collections & Technical Services
a division of the American Library Association
Chicago 2012

While extensive effort has gone into ensuring the reliability of information appearing in this book, the publisher makes no warranty, express or implied, on the accuracy or reliability of the information, and does not assume and hereby disclaims any liability to any person for any loss or damage caused by errors or omissions in this publication.

The paper used in this publication meets the minimum requirements of American National Standard for Information Sciences—Permanence of Paper for Printed Library Materials, ANSI Z39.48-1992.

Library of Congress Cataloging-in-Publication Data

Brown, Elizabeth (Elizabeth Anne)
Sudden selector's guide to chemistry resources / Elizabeth Brown.
pages cm. — (ALCTS/CMS sudden selector's series ; #3)
Includes bibliographical references.
ISBN 978-0-8389-8591-5
1. Chemical libraries—Collection development. 2. Chemistry—Bibliography—Methodology. I. Title.
Z675.C47B76 2012
025.06'54—dc23 2011042994

ISBN-13: 978-0-8389-8591-5

Printed in the United States of America

16 15 14 13 12 5 4 3 2 1

CONTENTS

FOREWORD

Is subject-area knowledge for collection development still necessary or even important in these days of tightening budgets, vendor selection, and nearly-instant access? My answer is a resounding "Yes!" It is vital for selectors to have an understanding of how their subjects "work," in terms of research, publication, and selection; selectors link a library's collection to its local audience, meeting the needs of researchers and faculty as well as the broader community. Selection by vendors, in the form of approval plans, can indeed create workflow efficiencies, but it takes a knowledgeable selector to set up an effective plan that can account for local needs as well as budgetary and space restrictions. The time saved by such plans allows selectors to both hone the margins of a collection to strengthen it, and to conduct increasingly valuable liaison work with user groups. The ongoing purpose of the Sudden Selector series is to provide current information on selection in specific subject areas, to assist selectors in creating a manageable process in unfamiliar subject territories.

Helene Williams
Editor, Sudden Selector's Guide Series
March 2012

PREFACE

On the Sudden Selector's Series

The Sudden Selector series was created by the Collection Management Section (formerly Collection Management & Development Section) of the Association for Library Collections & Technical Services division of the American Library Association. It is designed to help library workers become acquainted with the tools, resources, individuals, and organizations that can assist in developing collections in new or unfamiliar subject areas.

These guides are not intended to provide a general introduction to collection development but to quickly furnish tools for successful selection in a particular subject area. However, there are many tools that are pertinent for all subject areas and although not explored in detail in the guides, the following should be mentioned.

GUIDES TO COLLECTION DEVELOPMENT

Evans, G. Edward, and Margaret Zarnosky-Saponaro. *Developing Library and Information Center Collections*, 3rd ed. Westport, Conn.: Libraries Unlimited, 2005.

Authority on all areas of collection development, from user assessment, collection development policies, evaluation, deselection, and legal issues. This popular resource, in its many editions, has served as a standard text in collection development training.

Johnson, Peggy. *Fundamentals of Collection Development and Management*, 2nd ed. Chicago: American Library Association, 2009.

This guide by one of the key authorities in collection development covers many of the same areas as Evans and Edward. Johnson provides a comprehensive overview of the issues such as policies, planning, developing and managing collections, marketing and outreach activities, and collection analysis. The writing is engaging and its information is useful for both beginning professionals and seasoned selectors.

Disher, Wayne. *Crash Course in Collection Development*, Libraries Unlimited, 2007.

This title is part of the Crash Course series from Libraries Unlimited, and is aimed toward a new selector without any selection experience or for those with little to no professional experience. Although the general concepts covered may be useful for beginning academic librarians, it is focused toward the needs of public librarians.

Gorman, G. E., and Ruth H. Miller. *Collection Management for the 21st Century: A Handbook for Librarians*. Westport, Conn.: Libraries Unlimited, 1997.

Although a bit older than the other texts in this list, the essays address many crucial issues and challenges still of critical concern in collection development. The handbook provides a thorough review of the trends and emerging issues in the field.

Burgett, James, John Haar, and Linda L. Phillips. *Collaborative Collection Development: A Practical Guide for Your Library*. Chicago: American Library Association, 2004.

This guide provides first-hand experience and advice for successful collaborative collection building. The guide provides models and strategies for research, budgeting, promotion, and evaluation.

Alabaster, Carol. *Developing an Outstanding Core Collection: A Guide for Libraries.* Chicago: American Library Association, 2002.

This handbook provides instructions on how to build an adult public library collection from the ground up as well the tools to maintain an existing collection. The guide provides a wealth of resources for public library collection development as well as sample core lists.

REVIEW SOURCES

Choice
www.ala.org/ala/acrl/acrlpubs/choice/home.cfm

Reviews in *Choice* magazine, published monthly by the American Library Association, and *Choice Reviews Online* are targeted to academic library collections and reviews emphasize the importance of the title in collection development and scholarly research. *Choice* includes approximately 600 reviews (per month) organized by subdiscipline for books, electronic media and internet resources and as well as publisher advertisements and announcements for new and forthcoming publications. *Choice Reviews Online* provides access to issues from 1998 to the present. There are added features to the online version of the magazine including personalized profiles and title lists and an advanced search screen.

Library Journal Book Reviews
www.libraryjournal.com/community/Reviews/47110.html

Library Journal Review Alerts
www.libraryjournal.com/info/CA603597.html

Library Journal magazine provides brief reviews of titles on all topics and is aimed for both public and academic libraries. The reviews provide a brief summary of the title and recommendations for library audience and selection. Reviews are available in print issues of the magazine and online through various databases and as an RSS feed for new review title alerts.

Booklist
www.ala.org/ala/booklist/booklist.htm

www.booklistonline.com/

Booklist, a publication of the American Library Association, publishes over 8,000 recommended-only reviews of books, audio books, reference sources, video, and DVD titles each year. *Booklist* also provides coverage of ALA award winning titles and is available online with enhanced content such as advanced searching options and personalized profiles and lists.

Publisher's Weekly
www.publishersweekly.com/

This magazine is also available through an online subscription and serves as a trade publication for professionals in the library and publishing fields. Its coverage includes industry news, trends, events and book reviews. More than 7,000 book reviews are published annually and written by both freelance reviewers as well as well-known authors. The reviews are divided by fiction and non-fiction.

ELECTRONIC DISCUSSION LISTS AND WEB SITES

ACQNET-L
http://serials.infomotions.com/acqnet/

ACQNET serves as a moderated forum for the discussion of any topic of interest to acquisition librarians and other library professionals involved in acquisitions of all types of materials. The listserv maintains a searchable archive.

COLLDV-L
http://serials.infomotions.com/colldv-l/

COLLDV-L includes issues of acquisition but also covers more broad issues of collection management, such as policy development, deselection issues, and collection evaluation. It is a moderated discussion directed towards library collection development professionals, bibliographers, selectors, and others involved with library collection development.

ERIL-L
http://listserv.binghamton.edu/archives/eril-l.html

ERIL-L's purpose is to cover all aspects of electronic resources in libraries. In addition to collection management librarians, participants include reference personnel, systems librarians, and vendors with topics ranging from usage statistics to product issues to licensing. The list is moderated and archived.

Association for Library Collections & Technical Services (ALCTS) Collection Management Section (CMS)
www.ala.org/alcts/mgrps/cms

The purpose of CMS is to contribute to library service and librarianship through encouragement, promotion of, and responsibility for those activities of ALCTS relating to collection management and development, selection, and evaluation of library materials in all types of institutions. The section develops publications, online courses, and other tools for the training and further development of collection management.

ACQWEB
www.acqweb.org

Although the web site has not been recently updated and is under revision, it is still valuable in providing links to publisher and vendors as well as to other online resources of interest to acquisitions and collection development librarians.

This list is not meant to be exhaustive, but simply an introduction to some of the resources available for getting up to speed in collection development. As the Sudden Selector guides are subject-specific, most of the above resources are too general for inclusion in the main text. However, personnel responsible for collection development should ultimately be familiar with most of them. Additionally, for the most exhaustive bibliographies for further research, consult the guides to collection development listed above.

Doug Litts
Smithsonian Institution Libraries
American Art Museum & National Portrait Gallery
Editor, Sudden Selector's Guide Series, 2006–2009
Updated 2011

INTRODUCTION AND OVERVIEW

This guide is intended to serve as an introduction for new library selectors in chemistry. It is expected that a new chemistry selector will have had some training or academic background in the sciences. It is also expected that the new selector will have a basic understanding of reference and instructional skills as well as experience with answering reference questions or consulting individually with library users to determine their information needs. If not, then there is readily available background material, such as textbooks and reference guides, described in more detail in chapter one.

The guide is not intended to serve as a comprehensive guide to the chemical literature or chemical literature searching. Several volumes exist in the literature, and these sources can provide more extensive information on the history of chemical information, additional sources to consider for selection and literature searching, and other useful information.

Gary Wiggins, *Chemical Information Sources*, McGraw-Hill Series in Advanced Chemistry (New York: McGraw Hill, 1991).

Considered the most comprehensive and informative text on chemical information sources, this text has sections on all major areas of chemical information, including types of searches, and library materials. Particularly important are sections on patent searching, chemical properties, and chemical reactions geared to the perspective of a scientist. While many technology applications have changed since publication, the organization and information on each topic is relevant today. Updated information is available at the Chemical Information Sources wiki, annotated later in this text.

Robert E. Maizell, *How to Find Chemical Information: A Guide for Practicing Chemists, Educators, and Students*, 3rd ed. (New York: Wiley, 1998).

This title takes a different approach, describing chemical information topics from the perspective of the librarian. *Chemical Abstracts* and other indexes are covered, as well as major reference source types, journals, patents, property data, chemical industry information, and analytical data such as spectra.

R. T. Bottle and J. F. B. Rowland, eds., *Information Sources in Chemistry*, 4th ed. (New York: Bowker-Saur, 1993).

While older and less comprehensive than the previous titles, this volume contains concise descriptions of major topics in chemical information sources. Its focus on U.K. publications and perspective on patents, intellectual property, and chemical industry issues is unique.

This selector's guide is intended to serve several purposes. It is intended to serve as a brief introduction to the most useful sources for new selectors to utilize in their daily activities. Chapters are organized by activity to correspond with the daily practice of collections librarians. Material is also organized by format in order to show relationships between different online and print sources.

Many new selectors are required to learn a subject quickly and begin selecting material in a short time. The length of this volume ensures that a new selector can obtain the most relevant information for obtaining selection information and quickly connect to the most knowledgeable information professionals. Another goal of the guide is to show newer information sources not available in some of the more comprehensive texts above.

While the guide is intended to serve several needs, it is not intended to serve as an overall guide or textbook on collection development principles.

This information can be found in textbooks on this aspect of librarianship, several of which are mentioned in the preface.

This guide is also not intended to serve as a tutorial or textbook on chemistry or a specific field of chemistry. There are many excellent textbooks published on all areas of chemistry. Some of these are mentioned in chapter one. Introductory general chemistry textbooks are an excellent overview of chemistry topics, terminology, concepts, and scientists. General chemistry textbooks also provide a rich source of definitions as well as photos of chemical principles. The following selected titles are popular in many academic programs.

Steven Ebbing and Darrell Gammon, *General Chemistry*, 9th ed. (Boston: Houghton Mifflin, 2009).

Steven S. Zumdahl and Susan A. Zumdahl, *Chemistry*, 8th ed. (Boston: Houghton Mifflin, 2008).

Theodore, H. Brown, Eugene Lemay, Bruce E. Bursten, Catherine Murphy, and Patrick Woodward, *Chemistry: The Central Science*, 12th ed. (Upper Saddle River, NJ: Pearson, 2011).

ORGANIZATION OF THIS GUIDE

This guide begins with a general overview of the organization and practice in chemistry as background information to the selection process. This includes a description of the history of chemistry and how different areas of chemistry evolved, descriptions of the various types of library users that will utilize chemistry resources, how to analyze an existing collection of chemistry materials, and some strategies to begin selecting new material and working with library users.

The third chapter focuses on maintaining current awareness of the discipline as well as library activities at other institutions. Activities to successfully keep up with new information include contact information for library professional organizations, web resources, and social software tools to provide automatically updated content and book review sources.

Chapter 4 is a brief summary of the print chemistry literature, such as monographs, book series, handbooks, journal titles and conference proceedings.

Chapter 5 focuses on online databases and visual tools unique to chemistry including patents, technical reports, standards, safety data, spectroscopic information, chemical structure searching, and chemical nomenclature. The major literature indexes for chemistry are also profiled.

Chapter 6 details many of the activities required for successfully establishing and reviewing approval plan profiles for chemistry. These include reviewing existing plans with non-subject parameters in a profile and selecting publishers and book series. All of these activities are essential for effective fund management.

Chapter 7 provides general advice from an experienced selector on larger collections issues, such as time management strategies, keeping track of orders and requests, determining selection priorities with limited funds, and weeding and transferring materials.

one

Chemistry and Chemists

Chemistry is frequently referred to as "the central science," as many of the principles and concepts in chemistry overlap with other scientific disciplines such as physics, geology, biology, and engineering. It is defined as "That branch of physical science and research, which deals with the several elementary substances, or forms of matter, of which all bodies are composed, the laws that regulate the combination of these elements in the formation of compound bodies, and the various phenomena that accompany their exposure to diverse physical conditions."[1]

A second definition, and one which may be clearer, states chemistry is, "1) The science of the composition, structure, properties, and reactions of matter, especially of atomic and molecular systems; 2) The composition, structure, properties, and reactions of a substance."[2]

The history of chemistry and chemical discoveries is rich and colorful, beginning well before the recorded word as early cultures created substances from their surroundings for everyday use. One early example of this is soap, created from mixing tallow, an oil, with ashes, an alkali, or base. Systematic study of chemical principles began with the study of alchemy in the middle ages. Alchemy is the study of "A medieval chemical philosophy having as its asserted aims the transmutation of base metals into gold, the discovery of the panacea, and the preparation of the elixir of longevity."[3] Alchemy has its own colorful history and intertwines the study of the natural world with religion and magic. It served as a precursor to the discipline of chemistry we know today.

With the birth of the Renaissance and the development of scholarly learned societies, many chemical discoveries were made by individuals through experimentation and discussion with peers. Some well-known examples are the development of the laws of gases (Boyles's Law) and the elucidation of the role of oxygen in combustion (Laviosier). Theoretical ideas in chemistry came later, such as the development of chemical atomic theory (Dalton) and the creation of the Periodic Table (Mendeleev).

As experimentation and theory intermingled and the industrial age created more complex machinery for scientists to study chemical phenomena, chemists began to work in more structured laboratory environments and chemical discoveries became group activities. New areas of chemistry developed at this time include organic chemistry and physical chemistry. Other important discoveries include the determination of the structure of the atom and the development of quantum theory and quantum chemistry.

History of Chemistry

W. H. Brock, *The Norton History of Chemistry* (New York: Norton, 1993).

Provides a thorough historical overview of advances in chemical discoveries and theories.

Trevor H. Levere, *Transforming Matter: A History of Chemistry from Alchemy to the Buckyball* (Baltimore, MD: Johns Hopkins University Press, 2001).

Contains topical sections on major historical events in chemistry and the development of chemical research in the twentieth century, with a section on new frontiers in chemical research.

American Chemical Society Division of Chemical History, *ACS History Further Information*, www.scs.uiuc.edu/~mainzv/HIST/further/index.php (accessed March 22, 2012).

Provides links to historical information on chemistry and biographies of famous chemists.

As the science of chemistry becomes increasingly more specialized, applications of chemical principles to other scientific disciplines define today's research. Some examples of these applications include the growth of environmental chemistry, the development of polymers and polymer properties, and the creation of sensors and other chemical instrumentation to detect harmful substances.

MAIN SUBDIVISIONS OF CHEMISTRY

Chemistry traditionally has been subdivided into six main subdivisions. At the graduate level and above, chemists frequently specialize in one or more of these areas of research. Each area has its own history and traditions in the literature. The LC classification scheme for chemistry (QD) parallels these areas, making identification of materials in subdivisions relatively straightforward.

Analytical Chemistry (QD71-145). The study of measurement of properties and phenomena in chemical processes and understanding the chemical nature of all matter. It addresses the questions of "what chemicals are present, what are their characteristics and in what quantities are they present?" Analytical chemistry frequently involves specialized instrumentation, experiments, and analysis software.

Analytical methods serve as identification tools for chemicals, separate mixtures of chemicals from each other, and serve as ways to quantify the amount of a chemical present in a substance. Many methods have acronyms and other specialized terminology, which an undergraduate analytical chemistry textbook can clarify; it can also define methods and instrumentation apparatus diagrams.

Douglas A. Skoog, Donald M. West, F. James Holler, and Stanley R. Crouch, *Fundamentals of Analytical Chemistry*, 8th ed. (Florence, KY: Brooks & Cole, 2003).

Inorganic Chemistry (QD146-196). Studies the properties and phenomena associated with inorganic compounds. Inorganic compounds are usually minerals and can vary tremendously in size and complexity. Any periodic table elements (except for carbon, which forms the basis of organic chemistry) can be present in an inorganic compound.

Current research in inorganic chemistry focuses on the synthesis, preparation, characterization, and analysis of inorganic substances. This can involve a variety of reaction types including main group elements, transition metal complexes, coordination compounds, organometallic compounds, and cluster compounds.

F. Albert Cotton, Geoffrey Wilkinson, and Paul L. Gaus, *Basic Inorganic Chemistry*, 3rd ed. (New York: Wiley, 1994).

Organic Chemistry (QD241-449). Studies the preparation, properties, reactions, and composition of chemical compounds containing carbon (C), hydrogen (H), or (C-H) bonds. Organic chemical compounds can contain other elements including nitrogen, oxygen, halogens, phosphorus, silicon, and sulfur. These chemicals are called heterogeneous compounds since they contain both organic and inorganic chemicals.

Organic chemical compounds also contain various types of functional groups including alcohols, ethers, aldehydes and ketones, enols, carboxylic acids, esters, amines, and phenols. Each functional group in an organic chemical compound has unique properties and chemical reaction types.

Preparation and identification of organic chemicals is a primary area of activity in the research literature. Other research areas include the study of natural products, organometallic chemicals, and polymers.

Francis A. Carey and Robert Guiliano, *Organic Chemistry*, 8th ed. (New York: McGraw-Hill, 2010).

Physical Chemistry (QD450-801). The study of macroscopic, microscopic, atomic and particulate phenomena in chemical systems and chemical substances. Some commonly studied areas of physical chemistry include thermodynamics, quantum chemistry, statistical mechanics and kinetics.

Some examples of research in the area of physical chemistry include studying the effects of intermolecular forces on the physical properties of materials, the speed at which chemical reactions happen (chemical kinetics), and how quickly materials conduct electricity.

P. W. Atkins and Julio De Paula, *Physical Chemistry*, 9th ed. (New York: W. H. Freeman, 2009).

Theoretical Chemistry (QD450-801). Makes mathematical predictions of chemical behavior and phenomena from previously observed experiments. Frequently this involves computational programming. Some examples of research include molecular modeling, molecular dynamics, molecular mechanics, and chemical kinetics.

Jack Simons, *An Introduction to Theoretical Chemistry* (Cambridge: Cambridge University Press, 2003).

Biochemistry (QP, QD). The study of chemical processes and transformations in biological systems, such as the human body or a plant. Cellular components such as proteins, carbohydrates, lipids, and nucleic acids are the most commonly studied research topics. Biochemistry relies upon experimentation and computation to study biological processes and how energy is created and transported throughout living organisms.

Albert L. Lehninger, *Principles of Biochemistry*, 4th ed. (New York: W. H. Freeman, 2005).

INTERDISCIPLINARY RESEARCH AREAS

There has been a tremendous growth of interdisciplinary research in chemistry documented in the literature. Many chemists also align themselves with these newer areas of research that lie at the intersection of different areas of the sciences. Some examples are described below with introductory texts listed for more details on the research area. New research journals, reference sources, and books dedicated to study of these disciplines will be advertised and promoted to chemists as well as librarians.

Green Chemistry. Study and design of chemicals, products, and processes that reduce the need for hazardous materials and substances. It covers all areas of chemistry and is primarily focused on industrial applications. These include "dry" reactions (ones that do not have solvents), water-based reactions (rather than organic chemical solvents which require more chemical clean-up), and the elimination of extreme heat or other conditions to run chemical processes.

Mike L. Lancaster, *Green Chemistry: An Introductory Text* (Cambridge: Royal Society of Chemistry, 2002).

Materials Science. Study of materials and the properties of matter and its applications to various areas of science and engineering. Commonly encountered materials are polymers, metals, composite materials, ceramics, semiconductors, and glasses. Research in materials science frequently characterizes the properties of these materials, the wear on materials (tribology), the flow of materials (rheology), and the mechanical behavior of materials.

William Fortune Smith, *Principles of Materials Science and Engineering*, 3rd ed. (New York: McGraw-Hill, 1996).

Nanotechnology. Study of applied processes and control of matter that are small in scale, usually on the order of one micrometer or smaller. Nanotechnology also refers to the creation of scientific devices on this length scale. It encompasses many scientific disciplines (chemistry, physics, engineering, and biology). Areas of study in nanotechnology include quantum dots, nanotubes, nanowires, and nanoparticles.

Bharat Bhushan, ed., *Springer Handbook of Nanotechnology*, 3rd ed. (Berlin; New York: Springer, 2010).

Polymers. Substances with repeating structural units, or monomers, connected by covalent chemical bonds. Polymers can occur naturally or be created synthetically. Research in polymers can take many forms and involve analysis of polymer properties or the effect of polymers upon natural and man-made environments.

Hans-Georg Elias, *An Introduction to Polymer Science* (Weinheim: Cambridge: VCH, 1997).

WHO USES YOUR CHEMISTRY COLLECTION?

About Chemists

Chemistry is a well-developed and highly specialized discipline and as such the Ph.D. is considered the entry point to a professional career. All research faculty members in university academic programs will have a Ph.D. and postdoctoral research experience. Occasionally research faculty members may have degrees and training in related fields (usually biology, physics, or engineering) if the department has interdisciplinary research programs. Most of the graduate students in chemistry graduate programs are in the department's Ph.D. program.

Many chemists begin their career in graduate school when they select a faculty research advisor. Graduate students perform research work under the direction and mentorship of their advisor early in their graduate career and take few classes after the first year of their program. As scientists evolve in their graduate career they begin by presenting posters at local, regional, and national meetings on their current research projects. With more research experience, they present talks at regional and national professional society meetings and publish scholarly research articles with their research advisor as the principal investigator. These scholarly articles form the basis of their Ph.D. dissertation.

After receiving a Ph.D., many chemists become postdoctoral associates in academia (usually at large research universities) or take positions in the chemical industry in management, administration, or research. Postdoctoral researchers continue to publish scholarly research articles with their postdoctoral advisor as the principal research investigator. Many postdoctoral researchers assume positions as faculty members at universities, colleges, and research institutes, and are then considered the principal investigator, primary author, or main contact person for their research publications.

Active chemistry faculty members in academic departments regularly attend professional meetings and serve professional societies in a variety of capacities. As researchers become more prominent in their fields they will frequently be asked to present seminars at other universities, deliver keynote lectures, and chair symposia in their research areas at professional society meetings. Prominent chemists usually become members of prestigious organizations such as the National Academy of Sciences (NAS) or the American Association for the Advancement of Science (AAAS), which include members from all areas of the sciences. The Nobel Prize in Chemistry is considered the most prestigious award given to chemists and is a significant mark of distinction.

Academic chemistry researchers publish the majority of their results as refereed journal and review articles. Many researchers provide chapters for monographic book series and write books in their research areas, although this is considered of secondary importance to scholarly journal article production. Industrial chemists publish patents and technical reports as the primary outlet for disseminating research information.

CHEMISTRY PROFESSIONAL SOCIETIES

Professional societies and organizations have a rich history in the study of science, and chemists are active in a number of organizations related to the study of chemistry. Chemists belong to organizations that complement their research interests and frequently belong to multiple societies that cover these research areas. Societies serve as "invisible colleges" for researchers in both industry and academia, and scientists frequently attend these meetings to meet with their peers and disseminate their work to a wider audience. In addition to providing an outlet for communicating research, societies serve a social function as well, providing career guidance and professional contacts for career advancement. Society meetings are also one of the few times that academic and industrial chemists meet together professionally, as chemists in the private sector have confidentiality agreements regarding their research results and are limited in how they can share their research with peers.

The American Chemical Society (ACS). The ACS is the largest scientific society with more than 160,000 members. It was founded in 1876 and is the most comprehensive scientific society for chemists. The ACS has 178 local geographical sections and 33 technical divisions which cover all areas of chemistry research, chemical education, and chemical information. In addition to promoting chemistry research, the ACS also promotes the discipline and practice of chemistry through nationally publicized events such as National Chemistry Week and the Chemistry Olympiad. The ACS holds two national conferences annually with additional annual or bi-annual regional conferences and local section programming. The ACS's trade publication, *Chemical & Engineering News*, is available on the web and also as a print publication.

ACS maintains a variety of RSS web feeds including updates on the ACS web site (chemistry.org), a summary rss feed for articles published in ACS publications, alerts for specific journals, and publications and patent information updates. RSS feeds are also available for each individual journal publication. The ACS's Author and Reviewer Resource Center includes information for journal publications as well as featured authors at http://pubs.acs.org/page/4authors/index.html (accessed March 22, 2012).

The Royal Society of Chemistry (RSC). The Royal Society of Chemistry is the United Kingdom's equivalent of the ACS. The RSC was formed in 1980 from the merger of four organizations: the Chemical Society (formed in 1841 and then named the Chemical Society of London), the Royal Institute of Chemistry (founded in 1877 as the Institute of Chemistry of Great Britain), the Faraday Society (covering physical chemistry, founded in 1903, and named in honor of Michael Faraday), and the Society for Analytical Chemistry (formed in 1874).

The organization of the RSC is similar to the ACS with thirty-five local sections and discipline-based divisions (Analytical, Dalton, Education, Faraday, and Organic). The divisions are further broken down into subject groups in each division. Fora cover broad areas of study in chemistry (Chemical Biology, Environment, Sustainability, and Energy, Materials Chemistry, Industry and Technology).

Chemistryworldblog, a supplement to the monthly Royal Society of Chemistry trade publication *Chemistry World*, serves as a forum for news, opinions and discussion about the chemical sciences at http://prospect.rsc.org/blogs/cw/ (accessed March 22, 2012). Blog comments are moderated by the editor. The Royal Society of Chemistry maintains RSS feeds for chemistry news and individual feeds for each published journal at www.rsc.org/Publishing/Technology/rss.asp (accessed March 22, 2012). *Chemistry World* Podcast, at www.rsc.org/chemistryworld/podcast/CWpodcast.asp (accessed March 22, 2012) contains profiles, interviews and discussions on the latest topics in science and chemistry.

Chemical Heritage Foundation (CHF). CHF is a non-profit U.S. organization devoted to the history of chemistry and chemical literature. It was originally created in 1982 as the Center for the History of Chemistry (CHOC) jointly by the University of Pennsylvania, the American Chemical Society, and the American Institute for Chemical Engineers, assuming its current name in 1992. The foundation web site contains numerous aids for a chemistry selector including publications, online exhibits, and library staff expertise.

Materials Research Society (MRS). Created in 1973, the society has more than fourteen thousand members from the areas of chemistry, physics, and mechanical engineering. MRS has annual spring and fall meetings with programming on a variety of topics in materials science and engineering. MRS members are academic and industry researchers in chemistry, physics, and mechanical engineering.

Your Audience

Understanding the local and virtual audience that will use a chemistry collection is essential before acquiring and selecting titles. Due to the broad interdisciplinary nature of chemistry research there are a variety of potential audiences and each group will have different needs.

DEPARTMENTAL FACULTY

Essential for any academic collection is the support for and awareness of collection strengths in the organization's research activities and programs. Detailed information on faculty members' research interests and current publications are available from the department's web site. Most graduate departments also publish a guide that is distributed to potential graduate students. This provides a wealth of information about the department with profiles of each faculty member, including citations to current research articles and projects.

A variety of research staff work in chemistry and other science departments to provide support for research and instruction activities, and may also require library assistance with their work. Support staff members may include instrumentation specialists that service machines frequently used for identifying chemical substances, such as the NMR specialist or STM specialist; machine shop staff members who create specialized mechanical fittings and fix mechanical lab equipment; electronics shop and IT support staff who provide web support for computing and electronics equipment used for research experiments; and glassblowers who create and repair laboratory glassware that is difficult to replace.

Departmental Curriculum, Mission, and Institutional Goals. The chemistry department's curriculum, departmental mission, and institutional goals will also influence collection building. The best ways to locate this information is to look at the university catalog, course listings, and program descriptions. Many departments may have a mission and institutional goals on the department's web site or in the program guide. If there is no information at the department level the broader academic division may have this information, i.e. the school or college where the department resides.

UNDERGRADUATES

The strength of an undergraduate student research program is another indicator of a chemistry department's use of the library collections. This information can be found from the department web site or from discussion with the department chair or library liaison. Undergraduate student researchers frequently need additional guidance in the research process, from selecting appropriate sources to identifying appropriate search strategies for their needs. Many undergraduates will be unfamiliar with library services such as interlibrary loan and document delivery. It may also be their first exposure to more complex literature databases and tools such as structure searching and identifying property, reaction, or spectral data.

INTERDISCIPLINARY PROGRAMS

Interdisciplinary academic programs make use of chemistry library collections. These programs are frequently listed on a department's web site or in the university catalog, or are included on the university's web site under broader academic categories, such as School of Arts and Sciences.

AFFILIATED RESEARCH CENTERS AND PROGRAMS

Many large academic institutions have affiliated research centers and specialized research programs located on or near campus. These research centers draw on the expertise of faculty research interests and frequently include partnerships with local industry or non-profit organizations. They are usually listed in the university's division of research or a similar administrative unit on campus, or listed in the university's online or print directory. These centers frequently rely heavily on the academic library for research support.

LOCAL BUSINESSES AND CHEMICAL INDUSTRIES

Local businesses can also use academic library collections to supplement (or serve as a substitute for) their own corporate libraries. Increasingly, local researchers and businesspeople are using the academic library as their only source of research information. Frequently, affiliated users such as these serve as adjuncts or have informal research agreements with departmental faculty. Because of this, it may be difficult to determine a user's status and what library services are available to them. Special attention needs to be paid to ensure their access to the research literature does not violate the database use policies in the licensing agreement, specifically Chemical Abstract Service's (CAS) restrictions on academic institutions using Scifinder Scholar for for-profit research.

COMMUNITY USERS

Members of the wider community frequently use chemistry collections in academic libraries. These users can be local citizens looking for information for their children's science projects, people with a general interest in science, and local science teachers in primary and secondary education. Frequently these users are not familiar with an academic library's classification scheme or online access policies and may require additional assistance in the use of online sources. Some materials will not be available to them as they are not affiliated with the campus.

Reference Notes

1. J. A. Simpson and E. S. C. Weiner, preparers, *Oxford English Dictionary*, 2nd ed. (Oxford: Clarendon Press, 1989).
2. *The American Heritage Dictionary of the English Language*, 4th ed. (Boston: Houghton Mifflin, 2001).
3. *Ibid.*

two

Analyzing and Maintaining a Chemistry Collection

Taking an inventory of the strengths of your collection will show the weaknesses and gaps. There are several indicators of the strength of a chemistry collection. Some indicators will be external to the library:

- size of the department,
- number of active research faculty,
- number of faculty possessing prestigious awards in chemistry (such as Nobel Prize winners or fellows of societies such as the National Academy of Sciences),
- number of undergraduate and graduate degrees awarded by the department,
- age of the university—older universities will have larger historical collections of chemistry material,

- existence of a chemical engineering program—affects the number of volumes collected in chemical technology.

Some internal library factors that will help assess a chemistry collection include:

- level of funding for monographs and books,
- serials funding amounts and number of journals,
- existence of standing order funds for specialized book series,
- availability of specialized databases for searching the chemical literature (such as Scifinder Scholar and Reaxsys.)

FINDING THE STRENGTHS OF YOUR COLLECTION

The Stacks

The library shelves are often a rich source of information on collection strengths and use patterns, and much can be gleaned from browsing through the stacks and the online catalog in the call number ranges for chemistry and chemical technology. The reference collection, and bibliography collection, if one exists, will also give insight into the collection depth and strengths.

MONOGRAPHIC BOOKS

The presence of a variety of monographic book series in chemistry shows a commitment to ongoing expenditures in chemistry research titles. Monographic book series, described in more detail in chapter 4, have a rich tradition in the chemical literature and the presence of these titles shows that the library has invested in these titles consistently and with a concern for long-range planning.

MULTIVOLUME HANDBOOKS

Along with monographic book series, another indicator of strength of a collection is the existence of multivolume handbooks, such as Gmelin, Beilstein and Houben-Weyl. These large sets of print volumes and e-books, with dozens of volumes per set, chronicle the historical development and classification of chemical and biochemical reactions. Data included in these handbook series include the identification and classification of chemical substances and detailed chemical reaction information. These handbooks provide a multitude of chemical reaction and property data, and can provide historical data for many scientists' research needs.

TEXTBOOKS

The number and condition of both introductory and advanced level chemistry textbooks for undergraduate and graduate study is another indicator. These volumes are frequently among the most heavily used titles in a chemistry collection, and a wide range of well-worn titles indicates a heavily used collection.

Databases

CITATION DATABASES

Web of Science and abstract indexes to the chemical literature databases, such as Scifinder Scholar with additional subject indexes and online resources such as Reaxsys (formerly MDL Crossfire Commander, Beilstein Crossfire, and Gmelin Crossfire) show the strength of a library's chemistry collection and the level of support it provides to researchers.

Chemists are very conscious of citation counts and the popularity of their work among their peers, and resources with the ability to identify the top journals in a specialized area of chemistry, such as the Journal Citation Reports from Thomson Reuters or Scopus from Elsevier, may be requested of the library by either the academic department or university administration. Many chemists will compile lists and totals of the number of citations for their work for the promotion and tenure process. The existence of Web of Science or its equivalent in a pay-per-search database will be essential for this purpose.

PATENT DATABASES

Patent searching is also of interest to chemists, and the existence of patent information databases (either through free online sources or pay-per-search options) indicates an awareness of patent searching needs. Occasionally on large university research campuses this type of support is available from the research division or its equivalent. There may also be intellectual property support offices on campus or affiliated with the research division.

Scholarly Journals

Another indication of collection strength is the quantity and online availability of chemistry scholarly journals, either in addition to the print access or as electronic-only titles. Chemists are heavy users of the journal literature and use these titles for research much more often than books and conference proceedings. Journal titles can be from prominent scholarly societies such as the ACS and RSC as well as from smaller, more specialized societies and for-profit publishers. The mix of society to for-profit publisher titles can vary depending on the size of the collection and funding support.

CHALLENGES IN COLLECTING MATERIALS

Library materials in chemistry can range from popular works to very specialized research journals and books geared to a limited audience. The goal is to develop a balanced collection that will serve the broader needs of an academic institution and also provide adequate support for research activities and projects. This balance can be achieved by addressing the various challenges discussed below. In collecting for this subject it is essential to keep a balance between broad and specialized titles, and to collect both types of titles as funds permit.

One of the biggest challenges for any chemistry selector is the high cost of materials in chemistry and throughout the physical sciences (physics, geology, engineering, and mathematics). Books, research journals, online literature databases, and specialized information and research tools are frequently some of the most expensive to purchase and also require a high level of financial commitment to maintain access to material. Multivolume handbook series, topical monograph book series, and symposium series on standing orders can have a high degree of volatility, with higher publishing output in some years and less in others. Multivolume reference titles in chemistry are updated infrequently, and purchasing new editions can be challenging with a static collections budget.

A more recent challenge for the chemistry selector is incorporating new interdisciplinary areas of research into library collections. Since many of these newer areas of research lie outside the boundaries of traditional chemistry areas, more effort can be required to identify appropriate titles and build the collection. Some strategies are to work with other bibliographers to identify areas that overlap in collection building, and to exchange information on materials as needed. Searching book vendor title lists for the most popular titles purchased can also provide insight into new areas of research and overlapping collections areas.

COMMUNICATING EFFECTIVELY WITH CHEMISTS TO FACILITATE COLLECTION BUILDING

Effective communication with faculty and students in chemistry can seem like a daunting task. Chemists are often highly independent and self-educated on many topics, and the pace of scientific research often leaves them with little time for informal networking. In many academic environments chemists spend a typical workday performing experiments or supervising research projects during the day, with afternoon seminars or meetings as their primary means of networking. Scientists can also be solitary by nature and this can present special challenges to collection building.

For many new selectors a library liaison within a department is their first contact. This can be an effective way to communicate library issues and determine immediate collection needs but may not provide a means for developing longer-term collaborations with faculty members. Fortunately the activities of a chemistry department are usually well-defined, and there are activities that a new selector can participate in to meet faculty members and students.

If you are unfamiliar with chemical terminology or need help understanding concepts, identifying and sitting in on an introductory general chemistry or organic chemistry class provides an opportunity to learn concepts and meet students. A second place to meet chemists is at departmental colloquia seminars that are held throughout the academic year and also at undergraduate and graduate student poster sessions, usually held at the end of each semester. These meetings are open to all and scientists will be comfortable discussing their work with others in these settings.

Additional possibilities for reaching faculty members and determining their needs include offering reference service in the department's building, attending department meetings, and meeting with the department chair to discuss library and user needs. Other approaches to meeting faculty are through involvement on university and community committees and projects, especially for local chemistry activities such as National Chemistry Week or the Chemistry or Science Olympiad. Chemists frequently are involved in these activities and welcome new volunteers.

Communicating with chemists can be challenging since their research activities can be very specialized. Fortunately, scientists are frequently asked to explain their research to broad audiences and are able to describe their research clearly. Faculty who are receptive to new ideas, active on campus and community activities, have web sites with recent publications and research activity, and have an active research group, are some of the most receptive to meeting with librarians and other university staff. Taking the time to develop these relationships can be rewarding and provide much information on the needs of the department and improve the users' perception of the library's collections.

three

Keeping Up to Date

Keeping current as a selector on new developments and initiatives is no easy matter. It is especially difficult if one is new to a subject or has little knowledge of the literature and supporting materials. This chapter guides a new selector through many of these resources and support networks. The growth of new web technologies and social software applications has greatly increased options for networking with colleagues and using current awareness tools for publishing and scientific research.

PROFESSIONAL LIBRARY ORGANIZATIONS

The variety of professional organizations oriented to librarians and information professionals will broaden and enrich the practice of chemistry subject specialists. Each organization provides alternative approaches to conference programming and interaction with professional scientists and colleagues in the information profession. Organizations vary in size of membership, geographical dispersion of members, the level of specialization in the sciences, and understanding of chemistry collection needs.

Each professional organization provides a variety of valuable resources for any new selector. Experienced selectors will be available for advice and consultation on selecting titles and providing feedback on past practices for instruction and reference. Selectors in similar subject areas can also provide more general guidance on selection tools and planning for non-chemists' use of the collection. More general professional library organizations serve as a benchmark for emerging initiatives and to provide discussion of the philosophy and wider perspective of librarianship.

American Library Association (ALA). www.ala.org

The American Library Association (ALA) has a rich tradition in the library and information science profession. Formed in 1876 with more than sixty-five thousand members, it is the largest and oldest professional library organization. Within ALA there are membership divisions, round tables, affiliates, and chapters. The organization publishes a monthly magazine, *American Libraries*, and press releases on issues affecting the library and information science community.

Association of College and Research Libraries (ACRL). www.ala.org/acrl/ (accessed March 22, 2012); ACRL Science and Technology Section (STS), www.ala.org/acrl/aboutacrl/directoryofleadership/sections/sts/acr-stsec web site (accessed March 22, 2012).

The Association of College and Research Libraries (ACRL) is the largest division of ALA serving academic librarians with more than thirteen thousand members, seventeen sections, and forty-two local chapters. ACRL publishes a monthly magazine, *College and Research News*, as well as a peer-reviewed journal, *College & Research Libraries*, and holds biannual conferences, web casts, and virtual programming targeted to academic and special librarians on timely topics. The Science and Technology (STS) section of ACRL, formed in 1961, serves librarians in scientific and technical subject fields. This group will provide a new chemistry selector with access to selectors from chemistry and other areas of the sciences. STS publishes a newsletter, *The STS Signal*, and has extensive web site resources.

STS-L is the online discussion list, founded in 1994, with more than 1,100 subscribers. Membership includes members of ACRL STS as well as those interested in science librarianship. Discussion topics on the list include programming and STS committee project updates, news updates on publishing products in the sciences, and member announcements. The peer-reviewed quarterly, *Issues in Science and Technology Librarianship*, includes features on library users, collection needs, and the impact of new technologies on academic library practice, as well as news postings from ACRL. Other STS media includes ACRLog, a blog maintained by several members of ACRL, which contains posts on a variety of issues relevant to academic and science librarians. Postings are available from September 2005 to the present.

Special Libraries Association (SLA). SLA Chemistry Division (DCHEM), http://chemistry.sla.org/ (accessed March 22, 2012); SLA Science–Technology Division, http://scitech.sla.org/ (accessed March 22, 2012).

The Special Libraries Association (SLA), founded in 1909, represents more than eleven thousand information professionals in more than eighty countries worldwide with fifty-eight regional chapters, twenty-five discipline-specific divisions, and twelve interest-based caucuses. SLA's Chemistry Division, formed in 1966, has more than three hundred members in academic, corporate, and non-profit organizational settings. The division is concerned with the economics, educational advances, and information handling in the fields of chemistry and related subjects. This group has many materials to assist a new selector in chemistry, including the divisional newsletter, annual conference programming, continuing education courses, and extensive web site information with recent chemical research and publishing news.

SLA-DCHE is the online discussion list for the SLA Chemistry Division. It serves as a forum for division members to communicate division business and share announcements and publishing updates. Many members of the Chemistry Division are also subscribed to CHMINF-L, the ACS Division of Chemical Information discussion list, and broader discussion of issues in the profession and reference questions are directed there.

SLA's Science–Technology Division, formed in 1924, has more than one thousand members from all areas of science librarianship. The division draws SLA members concerned with applying the recording, retrieval and dissemination of knowledge and information in all areas of science and technology. The division produces a divisional newsletter, *The Sci-Tech News*, annual conference programming, continuing education courses, and web site resources. SLA-ST, the discussion list, has more than one thousand members and is archived back to 1997.

Topics include division information, activities, resource sharing, reference questions, reviewer or publishing opportunities, course and professional development opportunity announcements, research surveys, and science and technology library-related news.

American Chemical Society (ACS) Division of Chemical Information (CINF). www.acscinf.org/ (accessed March 22, 2012).

The CINF Division of the ACS is comprised of more than 1,400 members from academia, industry, and research. CINF membership and programming involves librarians, information professionals, and scientists concerned with chemical modeling and structure determination. With its diverse membership, conference programming usually includes symposia on chemistry library practice as well as the study of information modeling and structures. CINF publishes a bi-annual print bulletin, *Chemical Information Bulletin*, a monthly online newsletter, *CINF E-News*, and a web site with conference programming links.

CHMINF-L, founded in 1991, is one of the oldest and most established discussion lists for chemical information professionals and includes members of the ACS CINF Division and the SLA Chemistry Division. Membership includes librarians and information professionals from around the world, academic and corporate librarians, chemistry faculty and researchers with an interest in chemical information, and publisher representatives from the major chemical societies (ACS, RSC) as well as commercial publishers.

TOOLS, LINKS AND SELECTION AIDS

Social software technologies offer many additional online resources for a chemistry selector. New environments have been created for sharing information, monitoring online sites for new content, and communicating with colleagues and potential library users. A sampling of sources targeted to science and chemistry selectors is profiled below. Since this is a rapidly evolving area, new applications and sites will emerge and supply additional information that will not be included in the following lists.

Discussion Lists

Online discussion lists continue to remain a valuable virtual community for information professionals. Specialized online lists have developed within professional societies to discuss concerns including new products from publishers, mergers and acquisitions in the publishing industry, recent book reviews and online database products, and pricing and online access options for new and existing electronic products. In addition to the society discussion lists highlighted earlier, the following lists provide useful information on collection development concerns in chemistry and other subject areas. These lists are frequently targeted to specific tasks.

ERIL-L, http://listserv.binghamton.edu/archives/eril-l.html (accessed March 22, 2012).

Begun in 2005 and now with more than 1,800 members, the Electronic Resources in Libraries (ERIL) subscriber list includes staff from all library departments. Discussion topics include collection development policy, electronic journal holdings, usage statistics, licensing, product set-up and maintenance, ERM development, instruction, and specific product issues, job announcements, news items, and general announcements.

LIBLICENSE-L, http://liblicense.crl.edu/discussion-forum/ (accessed April 30, 2012).

Hosted by Yale University Library, the Commission on Preservation & Access, and the Council on Library Resources (CLIR) since 1997, this unmoderated list covers electronic content licensing for academic and research libraries. List discussions center on drafting library and educational license agreements for digital information content, insuring that license agreements do not inordinately restrict the use of digital information, and reconciling license agreements with fair use provisions of the U.S. Copyright Act. The Liblicense-L web site includes many additional resources for selectors including links to author and publisher licensing sites, a glossary of licensing terminology, and licensing initiatives in countries outside the U.S.

Blogs

Blogs provide an online diary or dialogue with an outside audience. Organizational blogs frequently serve as a tool to promote services and products, provide updates to title changes and access to products, and act as an outlet for press releases and other information. Publishers, librarians, scientists, and libraries all publish blogs, and the selection here represents a cross-section of activity at the time of this writing.

LIBRARIANS, LIBRARIES, AND RESEARCHERS

Drexel University Library, *Engineering Resource*, www.library.drexel.edu/blogs/englibrary/, (accessed March 22, 2012).

Authored primarily by Jay Bhatt, this blog lists new print and electronic resources available from the Drexel University Libraries and includes new and useful web resources on primarily engineering-related information topics. Postings are available from February 2005 to the present.

John Dupuis, *Confessions of a Science Librarian*, http://scienceblogs.com/confessions/ (accessed March 22, 2012).

This weblog by John Dupuis, Head of Steacie Science & Engineering Library at York University in Toronto, features links of interest to academic science librarians including collections, publisher updates, and science policy. Posts are available from October 2002 to the present.

OA *Librarian*, http://oalibrarian.blogspot.com/ (accessed March 22, 2012).

Maintained by several librarians; contains updates on open access news. Postings are available from January 2005 to the present.

Christina Pikas, *Christina's LIS Rant*, http://scienceblogs.com/christinaslisrant/ (accessed March 22, 2012).

This blog covers library and information science, scholarly communications, and science librarianship concerns from the perspective of a practicing librarian and LIS graduate student researcher. Emphasis is on observation and measurement of user behavior and the practice of science online. Coverage is from May 2009 on the Science Blogs web site.

Peter Murray-Rust, *petermr's blog*, http://blogs.ch.cam.ac.uk/pmr (accessed March 22, 2012).

Postings from Peter Murray-Rust on chemistry content on the Internet, open access initiatives, and other material. Content is available from September 2006 to the present.

Dorothea Salo, *Book of Trogool*, http://scientopia.org/blogs/bookoftrogool/ (accessed March 22, 2012).

Covers recent developments in cyberinfrastructure, open access, data curation, e-research, and science policy from July 2009 onwards, with an emphasis on technology and implications for the practice of librarianship.

University of Massachusetts, Amherst, *ISEL Update*, http://scilibupdate.blogspot.com/ (accessed March 22, 2012).

Contains news and discussion on information sources and library services targeted to science and engineering; compiled by the librarians at the University of Massachusetts Amherst's Integrated Sciences & Engineering Library (ISEL). Separate RSS feeds are available for postings in each discipline. Blog features cover publishing press announcements for new products and services as well as general interest science announcements and information. Blog features date from August 2005 to the present.

Useful Chemistry, http://usefulchem.blogspot.com/ (accessed March 22, 2012).

Maintained by several scientists, this is an open notebook science project in chemistry. Posts on specific problems and solutions in chemistry make up the majority of postings. Coverage is from July 2005 to the present.

PUBLISHERS

Library Journal, *Blogs on Library Journal*, www.libraryjournal.com/blogs.html (accessed March 22, 2012).

Library Journal maintains a variety of blogs on its web site. Each provides a different perspective on publishing and acquisition of materials for libraries.

Nature, *In the Field*, http://blogs.nature.com/ (accessed March 22, 2012).

Offers readers of *news@nature.com*, Nature's news site, and Nature Podcasts listeners an opportunity to comment on stories and events. Coverage is available from January 2006 to the present.

Nature, thescepticalchymist, http://blogs.nature.com/thescepticalchymist/ (accessed March 22, 2012).

This blog by the editors of *Nature* and the research journals serves as a forum for readers, authors and the entire chemical community. New discoveries and advances in chemistry and chemical biology are profiled, using the journal literature as well as news reports. A variety of authors provide postings on topics in all subfields of chemistry. Postings are available from March 2006 to the present.

Scientific American, *Sciam Observations*, http://blogs.scientificamerican.com/ (accessed March 22, 2012).

This blog offers opinions, arguments and analyses from the editors of *Scientific American* on a variety of topics. Postings are from September 2006 to the present.

PUBLISHER AND PUBLICATION RSS FEEDS

Chemical Abstracts Services, *News from CAS*, www.cas.org/feed.rss (accessed March 22, 2012).

The Chemical Abstracts Service offers a general news feed, with updates to information on CAS products, including Scifinder Scholar and Chemical Abstracts.

Elsevier, *Science Direct News*, www.sciencedirect.info/news/ (accessed March 22, 2012).

Elsevier maintains feeds through its Science Direct web site. SD Connect is an online news update service, and there is also a new title alert feed for all Science Direct titles.

John Wiley RSS Feeds, www.wiley.com/WileyCDA/Section/id-302565.html (accessed March 22, 2012).

Feeds for new title alerts for all areas in the sciences as well as a separate feed for reference titles, individual journal titles and a general newsletter for journal update information from John Wiley and Sons.

Nature, *Nature Web Feeds*, www.nature.com/webfeeds/index.html (accessed March 22, 2012).

Extensive list of feeds for the journal *Nature*, including highlights from China, Japan, current issue highlights, and news digest. Feeds are available for individual journals.

Science/AAAS, *RSS Feeds*, www.sciencemag.org/rss/ (accessed March 22, 2012).

The official publication for the Association for the Advancement of Science (AAAS) has feeds for *Science* magazine content including weekly news summaries, table of content information, and podcasts.

Science News, *RSS Feeds–Science News*, www.sciencenews.org/view/page/id/45/title/syndication (accessed March 22, 2012).

RSS feed for current articles and features from *Science News*, a weekly newsmagazine.

Scientific American, *Science News RSS Feed*, www.scientificamerican.com/page.cfm?section=rss (accessed March 22, 2012).

Provides RSS feeds on a variety of topics including global science matters, technology, health, nature, biology, space, and archeology, and a blog for commentary on science developments.

Springer, *RSS Journals, Books & Academic Online Media*, www.springer.com/alert/rss?SGWID=0-40691-0-0-0 (accessed March 22, 2012).

New title listings for science, social science, and humanities disciplines from Springer.

FACEBOOK AND SOCIAL NETWORKING SITES

Social networking sites have created even more opportunities for selectors to form communities with colleagues to share information and keep abreast of new titles and products from publishers. Social networking sites also allow selectors to interact with their potential audience including students, researchers, faculty, and the local community. The most popular social networking site for many academic and subject specialists in chemistry, Facebook, identifies individuals and groups of people with common interests. Other social networking sites, such as Friendfeed and Mendeley, count librarians, information professionals, and scientists as members, and new networks for the scientific community continue to emerge.

The following list is a sample of the ways information professionals have adapted this new technology to enrich the library experience and form new collaborative partnerships. One limitation of Facebook and many other new social software applications is the fluid nature of the medium. Many groups and initiatives develop quickly with new groups and applications being introduced, sometimes on a daily basis.

Discussion of the Sciences and their Philosophical Implications, www.facebook.com/groups/2204860879/ (accessed March 22, 2012).

Focuses on the discussion of various theories in the sciences, including news updates, photos, and discussion on a number of topics.

Knovel, www.facebook.com/Knovel?ref=ts (accessed March 22, 2012).

This vendor-based group has videos of demonstrations of e-book content available from a variety of science and technical handbooks. Also provides discussion of features and instructions on specialized search techniques.

Organic Chemistry, www.facebook.com/pages/Organic-Chemistry/107942725900764?sk=wiki (accessed March 22, 2012).

Serves as a knowledge base for organic chemistry and chemists.

Public Library of Science (PLoS), www.facebook.com/PLoS.org (accessed March 22, 2012).

News on recent editorial and policy developments in access to taxpayer-funded research.

SciTech Librarians, www.facebook.com/groups/2322018240/ (accessed March 22, 2012).

Includes librarians from all areas of science, technology, and medicine and discussion on a variety of topics in science and technology librarianship issues.

PORTAL WEB SITES

The following web sites are excellent gateway sources to many areas of chemistry collections and practice.

Indiana University, Bloomington, *Cheminfo: Chemical Information Sources from Indiana University, Bloomington*, www.libraries.iub.edu/index.php?pageId=78 (accessed March 22, 2012).

Considered the most complete academic web sites for chemistry re-sources. Instructional material includes sample class exercises, lists of reference and research sources, and information on online access to the chemical literature.

University of California, Berkeley, *Chemistry and Chemical Engineering Library, University of California at Berkeley*, www.lib.berkeley.edu/CHEM/ (accessed March 22, 2012).

Contains details on accessing chemical literature databases, course information, citation management software, patent information, and journal title abbreviations.

University of Chicago, *Chemistry Resources at the John Crerar Library, University of Chicago*, guides.lib.uchicago.edu/chemistry (accessed March 22, 2012).

Includes information on locating journal articles and print books in the library as well as links to other specialized information sources.

University of Texas at Austin, *Mallet Chemistry Library, University of Texas, Austin*, www.lib.utexas.edu/chem/ (accessed March 22, 2012).

General information and user guides for print and online sources, including an FAQ and other detailed information on tools including Scifinder Scholar, Beilstein and Gmelin online. Links to specialized sources such as handbooks, chemical properties, and Material Data Safety Sheets are included. Also contains the locally produced Thermodex index to thermodynamic data and a link to genealogy of the Chemistry Department of the University of Texas at Austin.

Open Science Project, www.openscience.org/blog/ (accessed March 22, 2012).

A collection of free and open tools for chemistry research and mathematical applications, the site is organized by subject areas and application, with chemistry highly represented.

WIKIS

Chemical Information Sources Wiki, http://en.wikibooks.org/wiki/Chemical_Information_Sources (accessed March 22, 2012).

Although this site is no longer being updated, original material was based on the print edition of *Chemical Information Sources* by Gary Wiggins. While the focus of this wiki is instruction and information for chemists, selectors will find links to materials and advice on acquiring a variety of chemistry resources. The wiki also includes the Clearinghouse for Chemical Information Instruction Materials, based at Indiana University, which lists sources and instructional materials for chemistry and science selectors.

Open Babel:Open Source Chemistry Toolbox, http://openbabel.org/wiki/Main_Page (accessed March 22, 2012).

An open, collaborative project wiki for chemistry research applications. Includes sources to search, convert, analyze, or store data from molecular modeling, chemistry, solid-state materials, biochemistry, or related areas with applications on the web site.

Useful Chem Wiki, http://usefulchem.wikispaces.com/ (accessed March 22, 2012).

Online notebook and research tools for the Bradley group at Drexel University. Includes general information on Open Notebook Science and tools used to share research online.

PODCASTS AND MIXED MEDIA

Podcasts are an excellent way for a new selector to learn about research developments and ideas in chemistry. Collections of podcasts available for new selectors in chemistry range from library-oriented topics and discussion to updates on new ideas and research in chemistry and the physical sciences. In addition to these podcasts, there is a rich collection of course lectures and other classroom materials in this format. While not covered for this publication, a search of chemistry and university lectures in podcast applications such as iTunes will yield a plethora of additional resources for new selectors to learn about the field of chemistry.

Chemistry Podcasts at Podfeed, www.podfeed.net/tags/chemistry (accessed March 22, 2012).

Podfeed, a podcast search engine contains podcasts on all topics, including Chemistry and the Physical sciences. Content is geared to information sources and new developments in research.

Library Journal, Webcasts, http://lj.libraryjournal.com/category/webcasts/ (accessed March 22, 2012).

Podcasts are available with guest speakers discussing a variety of timely library topics, including digitization of content and the future of libraries and the profession.

Nature Publishing Group, chemistry@nature.com, www.nature.com/chemistry/podcast.html (accessed March 22, 2012).

Podcasts include interviews with Nobel Prize Winners, discussions on nanotechnology research, and summaries of new content for the chemistry community.

SECOND LIFE AND VIRTUAL NETWORKS

Three-dimensional virtual networks are an emerging presence among information professionals and library users. The most well-known virtual world is Second Life, created by Linden Labs, and focuses on social and networking activities to provide entertainment for users as well as an area to explore new ideas and networks. Although there are widely varying estimates of how many million residents there are in Second Life, there is no question that this environment continues to expand and evolve. Activities showing promise for collection development and understanding of science collection needs are highlighted below. The *Useful Chemistry* blog, mentioned earlier in this chapter, also provides links to Second Life discussion and research results for chemistry.

secondlifemolecules, http://secondlifemolecules.wikispaces.com/ (accessed March 22, 2012).

This wiki records locations where molecules are found in Second Life and is maintained by chemists active in the Second Life community.

BOOK REVIEWS

Book reviews are of invaluable help in the selection of new library materials. Written reviews as well as informal conversations with library colleagues frequently determine if an item is essential to a growing collection or a lower priority item. Reviews are available from both librarians and scientists. The scope of a review may vary by the source. Traditionally, publications oriented to librarians will have a broader description of the work and more information on the appropriateness for specific library audiences. Science publications will frequently describe more of the content in the book and judge the quality of the science and scientific approach.

Booklist, www.booklistonline.com/ (accessed March 22, 2012).

A publication of the American Library Association for more than 100 years, *Booklist* magazine publishes more than eight-thousand recommended-only reviews of books, audiobooks, reference sources, video, and DVD titles each year. Special topic issues provide coverage on popular genres, topics and themes. Full coverage of ALA award-winning titles including the annual Editor's Choice, Top of the List issue, and ALA Notable books is provided. There are also interviews, essays, columns to supplement the reviews. *Booklist* is available online with enhanced content such as advanced searching options and personalized profiles and lists.

A subscription to *Booklist* or *Booklist Online* or is required to access book reviews.

Choice, www.ala.org/acrl/choice/ (accessed March 22, 2012).

Choice, published by the American Library Association, reaches more than thirty-five thousand academic librarians and faculty. Reviews in both the print and online versions of *Choice* are targeted to academic library collections, and emphasize the importance of the title in collection development and scholarly research. Access requires a subscription to the magazine. *Choice Reviews Online* provides access to issues from 1998 to the present. Added features in the online version include personalized profiles, title lists and an advanced search option.

Library Journal Book Reviews, reviews.libraryjournal.com/ (accessed March 22, 2012).

Library Journal Academic Newswire archive, www.libraryjournal.com/csp/cms/sites/LJ/NewsLetters/AcademicNewswireArchive/index.csp (accessed March 22, 2012).

Library Journal provides brief reviews of titles on all topics and academic areas. Each review provides a brief summary of the title and recommendations for library audience and selection. Reviews are available in print issues and online through several databases and as an RSS feed for new review title alerts. Subscription to *Library Journal* is required to view the full text of reviews. Review Alerts are available for free. Top-selling titles in all academic areas are featured in each weekly issue of the Library Journal Academic Newswire, a free online news service for updates on library and information science initiatives. Different academic areas are profiled, with ordering information provided by YBP Library Services. Electronic alerts can be established, and issues are available online from November 2005 to the present.

Issues in Science and Technology Librarianship (ISTL), www.istl.org (accessed March 22, 2012).

A publication of the STS section of ACRL, *ISTL* provides electronic sources reviews. These in-depth reviews provide a thorough description of product features, usability, scope of information, and coverage. Recent products include subject index databases, e-book collections, and science-related web search sites. Access to reviews is free, and e-mail updates for new issues are sent to the science discussion lists regularly.

Journal of Chemical Information and Modeling (JCIM), http://pubs.acs.org/journals/jcisd8/index.html (accessed March 22, 2012).

JCIM, (formerly the *Journal of Chemical Information and Computer Sciences*), published by the American Chemical Society (ACS), provides software and product descriptions in each issue. Products include online subject indexes through different platforms, chemistry productivity software such as chemical and structural drawing programs, and electronic book content. Reviews are available in both print and online editions. Access to software descriptions requires a subscription.

Physics Today, www.physicstoday.org/ (accessed March 22, 2012).

Physics Today, a monthly publication of the American Institute of Physics (AIP), contains in-depth reviews. Written by scientists, each review has selection recommendations as well as a summary of the book and the quality of the science content. Also included are lists of recently reviewed and published titles in all areas of physics, applied physics, materials science, astronomy, and mathematical physics. Access to the reviews requires a subscription.

Science, www.sciencemag.org/books/ (accessed March 22, 2012).

Contains free weekly book reviews on all areas of science on its web site. Each review is extensive with cited references.

Scientific American, www.scientificamerican.com/department.cfm?id=recommendations (accessed March 22, 2012).

Scientific American has extensive lists of in-depth book reviews in all areas of science, as well as specialized lists of science titles. These include best-selling science books through amazon.com, science fair resource books, popular science favorites, and titles geared to children and teen readers. Electronic and print titles available from *Scientific American* are also featured. E-mail alerts are available for many of these specialized book title alerts. RSS feeds are available for monthly book reviews. Reviews are freely available.

Open Access and Funding Mandates

There has been increasing interest and activity in exploring and promoting alternative publishing models such as Open Access and establishing funding agency mandates to require deposition of research output. Keeping up-to-date in this rapidly changing area can be time-consuming. This selected list of sources provides summary information on recent developments from publishers, funding agencies, universities, libraries, and research centers. Chemistry is less well-established with these newer funding models and mandates and library users may have questions about these developments.

OPEN ACCESS

Directory of Open Access Journals (DOAJ), www.doaj.org/ (accessed March 22, 2012).

DOAJ provides an alphabetical listing of journals with open access publishing worldwide, and includes journals with both subscription and open access options for articles.

OAD wiki, http://oad.simmons.edu/oadwiki/Main_Page (accessed March 22, 2012).

Hosted by The Graduate School of Library and Information Science (GSLIS) at Simmons College, this wiki has a wealth of information on open access (OA) publishing titles, subject and data repositories, and emerging trends. It is regularly updated by the OA community and has an editorial board monitor posted content. It also contains the OA Tracking Project, a list of new developments. The project replaced a previous discussion list and web site, Open Access News, as the latest source for information on OA developments and policies.

Sherpa/RoMEO Home – Publisher Copyright Policies and Self Archiving, www.sherpa.ac.uk/romeo/ (accessed March 22, 2012).

Provides information on copyright policies and posting guidelines for preprints, postprints, manuscripts, and published versions of scholarly articles.

SPARC Enews, www.arl.org/sparc/publications/enews/index.shtml (accessed March 22, 2012).

The monthly newsletter from SPARC, the Scholarly Resources and Academic Resources Coalition, contains updates from policy, legislation, publications, and programming in the U.S.

FUNDING MANDATE RESOURCES

As of this writing, the sole major science funding agency in the United States requiring researchers to submit materials is the National Institutes of Health. The open access links above also provide information on legislative actions and activities on funding mandates.

PubMedCentral Homepage, www.ncbi.nlm.nih.gov/pmc/ (accessed March 22, 2012).

Homepage for the repository for deposited items from NIH-funded research projects. Information is also available on posting new items to the site and determining if publishers can automatically deposit items for authors.

University at Buffalo Libraries, *Legislation – Scholarly Communication – University at Buffalo Libraries*, http://library.buffalo.edu/scholarly/legislation/ (accessed March 22, 2012).

This library web site gives an updated overview of legislative issues affecting scholarly communications, such as pending bills, funding mandates from agencies, and executive orders.

four

The Print Chemical Literature

The traditional chemical literature, while historical in nature, is still of use to chemists and scientists in academia and industry. This chapter covers the print literature including monographs, book series, handbooks, scholarly journals, and conference proceedings. Emphasis is on core collection titles and establishing a base print collection for walk-in users in the community as well as students, researchers, and faculty. In most sections there are tools and other aids to quickly determine the scope and breadth of the print collection.

MONOGRAPHS AND BOOK SERIES

Monographs and continuing book series in chemistry are a long-standing tradition with multiple series covering major subdivisions of chemistry. Chemists are familiar with these series and frequently refer to them for background material on an unfamiliar topic and rely on updated volumes to provide a general overview of updates in a particular field. Many book series in chemistry are classed under a single call number with a general title and annual volume updates with subtitles. Other series have varying call numbers with volumes scattered in different locations.

There are few niche and small press titles in monograph series. These publishers include smaller chemistry and scientific societies and presses from outside the U.S., Western Europe, and Asia. These titles are not collected by many academic and corporate institutions and libraries. Due to the rapid publication of research material, few current bibliographies and treatises are available in chemistry.

GENERAL TREATISES

Joseph William Mellor, *A Comprehensive Treatise on Inorganic and Theoretical Chemistry, by J.W. Mellor* (London: Longmans, Green and Co., 1947).

Considered the standard treatise in chemistry, this set was first published in 1946. Additional supplemental volumes complement the original 16-volume work.

Henry Enfield Roscoe, *A Treatise on Chemistry, by the Right Hon. Sir H. E. Roscoe and C. Schorlemmer* (London: Macmillan, 1920).

First published in 1877, this shorter two-volume set focuses on the development of ideas and theories in chemistry.

Izaak Maurits Kolthoff, ed., *Treatise on Analytical Chemistry* (New York: Wiley, 1978).

This multivolume set encompasses the theory and practice of analytical chemistry.

Heinrich Remy, *Treatise on Inorganic Chemistry*, trans. by J. S. Anderson, edited by J. Kleinberg (New York: Elsevier, 1956).

This two-volume set covers all areas of inorganic chemistry. Chapters are organized by sections of the periodic table, and also by topics such as bonding, type of material (alloys, salts, etc.), and reaction types.

E. H. Rodd, *Rodd's Chemistry of Carbon Compounds; A Modern Comprehensive Treatise*, 2nd ed. (New York: Elsevier, 1964).

This series first edition appeared in 1951, with a second edition in 1964. Both multivolume sets are considered essential to the study of organic chemistry. Volumes are classed by functional group and reaction type. Supplemental volumes to the second edition update work from the earlier volumes.

J. R. Partington, *An Advanced Treatise on Physical Chemistry* (London: Longmans, Green, 1949-53).

This two-volume set covers experimental and theoretical developments in physical chemistry.

MONOGRAPH BOOK SERIES IN CHEMISTRY

Popular and long-standing monograph series in chemistry are listed below to help guide the new selector. Titles are grouped by publisher, including trade, university and professional society presses. Series can have a separate and individual volume title, or sequentially numbered annual volumes. Both series types are included in the lists in table 1.

TABLE 1

Academic Press/ Elsevier
Advances in Inorganic Chemistry
Advances in Carbohydrate Chemistry and Biochemistry
Advances in Heterocyclic Chemistry
Advances in Organometallic Chemistry
Advances in Protein Chemistry
Advances in Quantum Chemistry
Advances in Catalysis
The Alkaloids
American Chemical Society (ACS)
Advances in Chemistry Series
ACS Handbooks
ACS Monograph Series
ACS Symposium Series

Annual Reviews

Annual Review of Physical Chemistry
Annual Review of Analytical Chemistry
Annual Review of Biochemistry
Annual Review of Materials Research

Cambridge University Press (CUP)

Cambridge Environmental Chemistry Series
Cambridge Molecular Science
Chemistry of Solid State Materials
Cambridge Monographs in Physical Chemistry

(cont.)

TABLE 1 (cont.)

CRC Press / Taylor and Francis

Advances in Chromatography
Advanced Materials and Technologies
Advances in Metallic Alloys
Analytical Chemistry Series
Analytical Methods and Special Functions
Chemistry and Physics of Carbon
Chromatographic Science Series
Critical Reviews in Computational Chemistry
Drug and Chemical Toxicology
Electroanalytical Chemistry: A Series of Advances
Liquid Crystals Book Series
Materials Science and Technology
Modern Monographs in Analytical Chemistry
Molecular and Supramolecular Photochemistry
Monographs in Electroanalytical Chemistry and Electrochemistry
Nanotechnology Series
Organic and Bioorganic Chemistry
Organic Photochemistry
Series in Chemical Physics
Series in Materials Science and Engineering
Studies in Organic Chemistry
Undergraduate Chemistry: A Series of Textbooks

Elsevier

Studies in Natural Products Chemistry
Tetrahedron Organic Chemistry Series
Studies in Inorganic Chemistry
Advances in Carbohydrate Chemistry and Biochemistry
Advances in Catalysis
Advances in Heterocyclic Chemistry
Advances in Inorganic Chemistry
Advances in Quantum Chemistry
Advances in Organometallic Chemistry
Advances in Physical Organic Chemistry
The Alkaloids: Chemistry and Biology
Annual Reports in Computational Chemistry
Annual Reports in Medicinal Chemistry
Annual Reports on NMR Spectroscopy

Karger

Theilheimer's Synthetic Methods of Organic Chemistry (Synthetische Methoden der organischen Chemie)

McGraw-Hill

McGraw-Hill Series in Advanced Chemistry
McGraw-Hill Series in Chemistry
McGraw-Hill Handbooks

Oxford University Press (OUP)

Topics in Organic Chemistry
Topics in Environmental Chemistry
Practical Approach in Chemistry Series
Oxford Chemistry Masters
Oxford Chemistry Primer in Physical Chemistry
Oxford Chemistry Primer in Inorganic Chemistry
Oxford Chemistry Primer in Organic Chemistry
Oxford Chemistry Primer in Chemical Engineering
Oxford Chemistry Primer in General Chemistry

Royal Society of Chemistry (RSC)

Comprehensive Series in Photochemical & Photobiological Sciences
Monographs in Supramolecular Chemistry
RSC Analytical Spectroscopy Monographs
RSC Chromatography Monographs
RSC Materials Monographs
RSC Nanoscience and Nanotechnology Series
Tutorial Chemistry Texts

Springer / Kluwer

Advances in Polymer Science
Modern Aspects of Electrochemistry
Springer Series in Chemical Physics
Springer Series on Chemical Sensors and Biosensors
Structure and Bonding
Topics in Current Chemistry
Topics in Heterocyclic Chemistry
Topics in Medicinal Chemistry
Topics in Organometallic Chemistry
Fundamental and Applied Catalysis
International Tables for Crystallography
Lecture Notes in Chemistry

(cont.)

TABLE 1 (cont.)

Modern Analytical Chemistry
Modern Inorganic Chemistry
Nanostructure Science and Technology
Progress in Colloid and Polymer Science
Progress in Theoretical Chemistry and Physics
Surface and Colloid Science
Topics in Applied Chemistry

Thieme Publishers

Thieme Foundations of Organic Chemistry Series

John Wiley and Sons (Wiley)

Advances in Chemical Physics
Advances in Electrochemical Science and Engineering
Advances in Photochemistry
Analytical Techniques in the Sciences
Chemistry of Functional Groups
The Chemistry of Heterocyclic Compounds
Inorganic Reactions and Methods
Inorganic Syntheses
Methods and Principles in Medicinal Chemistry
Organic Reaction Mechanisms Series
Organic Syntheses
Perspectives in Supramolecular Chemistry
Progress in Inorganic Chemistry
Progress in Physical Organic Chemistry
Reviews in Computational Chemistry
Topics in Stereochemistry
Total Synthesis of Natural Products

World Scientific, Inc.

Advanced Series in Physical Chemistry
Advances in Multi-Photon Processes and Spectroscopy
Catalytic Science Series
Computational Chemistry: Reviews of Current Trends
Methods in Chromatography
Recent Advances in Computational Chemistry
World Scientific Lecture and Course Notes in Chemistry
World Scientific Series in 20th Century Chemistry
World Scientific Series in Nanoscience and Nanotechnology

PRINT AND ONLINE HANDBOOKS

Multivolume handbook series in chemistry have a rich history and several long-standing handbook series are featured in this section. Due to the high cost of individual print volumes and online availability, these handbook holdings are incomplete at many academic and corporate libraries. Nevertheless, these series provide a rich history of chemical reactions and the chemical literature not available in other sources. Many print volumes of these series were originally published in German, with recent volumes available in English.

Friedrich Konrad Beilstein, *Beilsteins Handbuch der Organischen Chemie (Beilstein Handbook of Organic Chemistry)* (Berlin: J. Springer, 1918-40).

Commonly referred to as the Beilstein handbook, this comprehensive series covers organic chemistry from before 1909 to 1979. Many institutions have online access to this handbook through the Reaxys interface, which will be described in more detail in the next chapter. Beilstein serves as an important reference tool because of both its historical scope and the depth of information collected on chemical substances.

Stephen Heller, *The Beilstein System–An Introduction*, www.hellers.com/steve/resume/p149.html (accessed March 22, 2012).

Provides a brief history of the Beilstein handbook and general overview of coverage in the series volumes.

William Armstrong, *Beilstein's Handbook Of Organic Chemistry: A Guide to the Printed Beilstein*, www.lib.lsu.edu/sci/chem/guides/srs147.html (accessed March 22, 2012).

This succinct and organized guide shows the organization, coverage, and structure of the print series volumes.

Leopold Gmelin, *Gmelin's Handbuch der Anorganishchen Chemie*, 8th ed. (New York: Springer-Verlag, 1926–1998).

Commonly referred to as Gmelin, this comprehensive multivolume set covers critically evaluated data in inorganic chemistry. Volumes are arranged by the Gmelin system of elements and compounds. Entries cover the history, occurrence, properties, methods of preparation, and commercial process of manufacture, with original literature references. There is an online database, Gmelin Crossfire, analogous to MDL Crossfire Commander, to search the printed volumes, which are in German. Gmelin Crossfire will be discussed in more detail in the next chapter.

William Armstrong, *Gmelin's Handbook Of Inorganic Chemistry: A Basic Guide*, www.lib.lsu.edu/sci/chem/guides/srs145.html (accessed March 22, 2012).

Covers the scope and organization of the series, as well as some naming conventions.

Josepf B. Houben, *Methoden der Organischen Chemie (Houben-Weyl Methods of Organic Chemistry)* (Stuttgart: G. Thieme, 1952-1999). www.thieme-chemistry.com/en/products/reference-works/houben-weyl.html (accessed March 22, 2012).

Commonly referred to as Houben-Weyl, this series comprehensively covers preparative methods in organic and organometallic chemistry. Methods are organized according to the class of compound or functional group to be synthesized. All known synthetic methods leading to a product class are covered in each individual volume, with a concise overview of the reactions. The series is now available online as the *Science of Synthesis* series, with individual titles available as e-books.

Thieme Publishing, History: Editions 1–4 (1909–1982), www.thieme-chemistry.com/en/products/reference-works/houben-weyl/format/original-series.html (accessed March 22, 2012).

Thieme provides information on the earlier print editions of Houben-Weyl and PDF lists of volume titles for each series.

Current Edition: Science of Synthesis (2000–), www.thieme-chemistry.com/en/formate/referenzwerke/science-of-synthesis.html (accessed March 22, 2012).

Started in 2000 and still in production, this newest edition of the Houben-Weyl series is available both in print and online, and is designed to provide the most up-to-date and comprehensive information on organic and organometallic chemistry.

PUBLISHING OUTPUT AND COST DATA

Publishing output in chemistry is lower relative to the humanities, social sciences, and other science disciplines. This is due to the high degree of specialization in chemical research and researchers relying more heavily on the journal literature for new ideas for projects.

YBP Library Services/Baker & Taylor, *Annual Book Price Update*, www.ybp.com/book_price_update.html (accessed March 22, 2012).

YBP provides annual book price update information for all Library of Congress classification codes. Since data is shown by LC call number, comparison with the social sciences and humanities is less straightforward than with other industry reports.

JOURNALS

The journal literature is tremendously important to scientists in academia and industry, and chemists are dependent upon peer-reviewed literature sources for disseminating advances in research among colleagues. Academic chemists monitor the citations produced from their own journal articles to measure the impact of their work. Chemists are also quite conscious of both the quantity of material published as well as the quality of the research. Online-only and electronic editions of journals are heavily used and are considered the primary route to view recent research activity. There is some tendency for more established researchers and those less active in research to prefer the print journal format.

The creation of online archives and backfiles of journal articles has also been heavily adopted for chemistry journals. The major chemical society publishers (ACS, RSC) have online archives of all content from their peer-reviewed publications. Online journal archives from many major commercial publishers (Elsevier, Springer, Thieme, and Wiley) are also readily available. The norm is to have online access back to before 1990. Very few, if any, journals remain in print. The physical sciences were early adopters of online journals and journal archives.

Journal publication models and changes in publisher distribution and editorial policies are ever-changing and complex. Overall, chemistry has been slower to adapt to newer publishing models such as open access, and chemists who participate in the publishing of peer-reviewed literature are reluctant to change traditional publishing models. Many of the major publishers have optional open access programs for authors. The ACS offers a version of open access called "Author Choice" in which authors pay to have an article published in return for a limited number of free web downloads.

Library Journal, Annual Periodical Price Survey, Annual Articles, www.libraryjournal.com (accessed March 22, 2012).

Library Journal's annual periodicals price report provides an excellent overview of trends in the costs and publishing environment for serials in all areas. Cost information, predictions, and trend forecasting for all areas of the sciences, as well as comparative information for the arts, humanities, and social sciences is available.

CORE CHEMISTRY RESEARCH JOURNALS

Compiling core journal titles in chemistry can be accomplished in several ways. Since chemistry is such a journal-dependent discipline, finding core titles in all areas of the field is not difficult. In addition to the lists compiled here, faculty and researchers at one's institution can be consulted to see if specialized or specific titles of interest are necessary. Due to the growth of interdisciplinary research and changing publishing models, new journals are frequently launched; in addition, distribution and publishing models can change from one year to the next. The best source of current information is from the web site of the journal in question.

American Chemical Society Committee on Professional Training (CPT), *CPT-Recommended Journal List*, http://portal.acs.org/portal/PublicWebSite/about/governance/committees/training/acsapproved/CTP_006024 (accessed March 22, 2012).

The Committee on Professional Training (CPT) of the American Chemical Society publishes lists of recommended journal titles for departments and libraries. This list is consulted when a department is evaluated for ACS accreditation of the undergraduate degree program in chemistry. The ACS CPT revised the Guidelines for Bachelor's Degree Programs and Supplement to Chemical Information Retrieval skills in 2008, and lists guidelines required for undergraduate majors in chemistry. See the appendix for more information on specific recommended journal titles. These ACS-recommended general content and topical journals are considered among the top journals in their areas.

Thomson Reuters, Journal Citation Reports–Science–Thomson Reuters, http://thomsonreuters.com/products_services/science/science_products/a-z/journal_citation_reports (accessed March 22, 2012).

This is the primary source for quantitative assessment of journals in all areas of chemistry. Each subdivision of chemistry (and other scientific disciplines) contains journal data and bases impact factor rankings on the number of citations per article in the publication. Many chemists consider Journal Citation Reports (JCR) an accurate reflection of the top journals in their area. Additional information such as change in impact factor and ranking is also included, indicating the journal's changing influence in the research area it represents. New journals are not always added immediately to Web of Science, so the impact factor may not accurately reflect the prestige and influence within the scientific community.

The appendix lists the highly cited journals in the main areas of chemistry and interdisciplinary science research areas in alphabetical order. The list was created to address different scenarios for new selectors. One scenario would be to determine the highest-priority journal titles and ascertain whether the core needs of chemistry researchers were being met. A second situation could be to analyze subdisciplines of chemistry and determine the number of core titles and coverage available in the collection. The strength of collections may vary between subdisciplines, and between libraries, and having lists of titles in each area makes this task much simpler. A third scenario would be to use these titles to supplement faculty input in serials review decisions.

Several other differences in the ACS and JCR title lists should be considered when looking at data. The ACS list is published less frequently than the Journal Citation Reports, and is also weighted more heavily towards American journal titles and ACS publications. The Journal Citation Reports include more interdisciplinary, international, and newer publications. One limitation of JCR data is that new journals are not added immediately, with a waiting period of a year or more before the journal is considered for inclusion. The Journal Citation Reports also measure additional quantitative criteria such as impact factor and cited half-life.

CONFERENCE PROCEEDINGS

Chemists often present research results at conferences and professional meetings, and these proceedings are published in both print and electronic formats. Since chemists are usually more interested in the peer-reviewed published results of research rather than conference proceedings, few proceedings are considered essential to many chemistry collections. Some of the most prominent collections of proceedings are listed here.

American Chemical Society, *Division Proceedings Online*, http://pubs.acs.org/meetingpreprints/index.html (accessed March 22, 2012).

These are papers collected from divisional programming events at the ACS national meetings. These are available in print as well as electronic subscription-based formats. Electronic access to proceedings abstracts is available in some cases through Scifinder Scholar and Web of Science, which will be covered in the next chapter.

American Chemical Society, ACS *Symposium Series* (ACS *Publications*), http://pubs.acs.org/series/symposium (accessed March 22, 2012).

The ACS publishes meeting papers from all society divisions through the ACS Symposium Series. Each numbered volume in the series has its own individual title and call number. Full listings of all symposia, as well as criteria and the publication process, is described in detail on the ACS web site.

Materials Research Society, *MRS Online Proceedings Library*, www.mrs.org/opl/ (accessed March 22, 2012).

The Materials Research Society provides bound and online volumes of proceedings from its biannual national meetings. Online packages are available for the entire collection of proceedings, or individual print volumes can be ordered directly through the publisher. Slide presentations as well as individual papers are available from the web site.

Royal Society of Chemistry, *Royal Society of Chemistry Book Catalogue*, www.rsc.org/shop/books, (accessed March 22, 2012).

Conference proceedings are published regularly from the Royal Society of Chemistry on many areas of chemistry. They can be found by searching the online book catalog at the RSC publishing web site.

five

Specialized Chemistry Research Tools

The chemical literature is a complicated environment, with many specialized sources that are searched through a complex array of tools. Documents such as patents and standards, chemical spectra, chemical safety data, complex chemical names, and intricate substance structures are frequently encountered in the chemical research literature. The ability to interpret and understand these specialized tools is critical to making prudent collection decisions. This chapter explores the tools that chemists and scientists utilize to explore the chemical literature and research, with special emphasis on explanatory and overview sources to guide a new selector unfamiliar with their use. In most cases these resources are unique to chemistry but may also be frequently encountered in engineering and other areas of the physical sciences.

Chemical information databases have historically been high-cost with access limited to better-funded academic and commercial industrial laboratories. For many institutions the chemistry literature indexes will be one of the most expensive purchases in the collections budget, with the exception of large bundled electronic journal packages. Historically, little chemistry research information was freely available to individuals and public library patrons. New web networking tools and the growth of newer publishing models have made more research articles and data freely available on the web. These free tools will be noted throughout this section as well as alternative purchasing options such as pay-per-search.

CHEMICAL RESEARCH LITERATURE

The rich history of peer-reviewed chemical research literature is documented through print indexes and online databases, handbooks, and web sites. Indexes covering chemistry and its allied areas are described in the most detail. Specialized chemical literature indexes are also profiled, and general science databases useful for collection building are included. For each bibliographic index, the extent of usefulness for interdisciplinary searching is also profiled.

Chemical Abstracts, *Chemical Abstracts Service*, www.cas.org/index.html (accessed March 22, 2012).

The Chemical Abstracts Service (CAS), a division of the American Chemical Society, creates the world's largest, most current, and comprehensive index to the chemical literature. CAS's databases are designed with a suite of searching options through several different platforms to locate chemical substances, chemical literature sources, chemical reaction information, commercial chemical sources, and chemical regulatory information. Because of this broad scope, the complexity of information indexed, and the amount of information indexed by staff at CAS, this is an expensive index and less likely to be found in a small academic institution or public library.

Chemical Abstracts is available online through several platforms designed for commercial, academic, and individual audiences. Scifinder, available to the commercial chemical industry, and Scifinder Scholar, available to the academic community, have both web and client search interfaces. Institutions may have either or both interfaces available for patron use. Pay-per-search accounts and packages are available to search Chemical Abstracts through a family of STN products including STN Express, STN Viewer, STN on the Web and STN Easy. Command-line searching of Chemical Abstracts (and many other science databases) is also available through the STN network (similar to the historical Dialog database network). Searching is also available through print volumes of *Chemical Abstracts*.

Scifinder

CAS, *Scifinder*, www.cas.org/products/scifindr/index.html (accessed March 22, 2012).

General information on Scifinder is included here, including licensing and access options. Features specific to Scifinder are listed at www.cas.org/products/sfacad/sfssfdiffers.html (accessed March 22, 2012). These include the current-awareness tool Keep Me Posted, the visualization and analysis tool Panorama, and the sequence searching tool BLAST.

Scifinder Scholar

CAS, *Scifinder Scholar*, www.cas.org/products/sfacad/index.html (accessed March 22, 2012).

Scifinder Scholar contains a portfolio of databases that are interlinked to support multiple searching options throughout the chemical literature. General information on Scifinder Scholar is included here, including support information, features, and content.

CAS, *SciFinder Scholar How To Guides*, www.cas.org/support/academic/sf/htg/index.html (accessed March 22, 2012).

CAS has created many user guides and support information for using Scifinder Scholar. Sessions are available for all levels of users, including new selectors. Scifinder and Scifinder Scholar contain five databases. Each one is described here with information on scope and how it is used in conjunction with other tools.

CAS, *CAplus Journal and Patent References*, www.cas.org/expertise/cascontent/caplus/index.html (accessed March 22, 2012).

CAplus is the core database in Scifinder Scholar and contains millions of indexed journal articles and patents on research in biomedical sciences, chemistry, engineering, materials science, and agricultural science. More than nine thousand journals are indexed and patent information is available from more than sixty countries. This database is used for general literature and patent searching.

CAS, *CAS REGISTRY – the gold standard for substance information*, www.cas.org/expertise/cascontent/registry/index.html (accessed March 22, 2012).

REGISTRY is an inventory of chemical substances from the patent, journal, and web literature. It contains more than fifty-three million substances and sity-one million sequences, and is used to identify a substance from the structure by importing the substance into CAplus for a literature search. REGISTRY can also locate property data, spectra, preparative methods, commercial availability, and regulatory information. Unique identifiers for substances, registry numbers, are cross-searchable with other databases within Scifinder Scholar.

CAS, *CASREACT, Chemical Reactions*, www.cas.org/expertise/cascontent/casreact.html (accessed March 22, 2012).

CASREACT provides reaction details including products, reactants, catalysts, reaction conditions and reaction yields. Results from this database also interlinks with CAplus and REGISTRY to provide literature sources and detailed substance information for reactions. More than 24 million reactions, 13 million preparations, and 750,000 journal articles with reaction information are available.

CAS, *CHEMCATS, Commercially Available Chemicals*, www.cas.org/expertise/cascontent/chemcats.html (accessed March 22, 2012).

CHEMCATS includes information on common and specialty commercially available chemicals. It links with the substance and reaction databases REGISTRY and CASREACT.

CAS, *CHEMLIST, Regulated Chemicals Information*, www.cas.org/expertise/cascontent/regulated/index.html (accessed March 22, 2012).

CHEMLIST contains information on regulations for specific chemicals, such as environmental, poisonous or other potentially harmful substances. More than 250,000 substances are included and linked with the REGISTRY database.

CAS, *Scifinder Content at a Glance – Biomedical Information*, www.cas.org/expertise/cascontent/ataglance/medlinecontent.html (accessed March 22, 2012).

Information is included on the scope and content of Medline within Scifinder Scholar. Medline is used primarily to search biochemical and biology applications concurrently with Chemical Abstracts within Scifinder Scholar.

STN, STN Express, STN Easy, STN Viewer, STN on the Web

The STN database collection covers many areas of the sciences and technology through a web or client command-driven interface. Access to STN requires an account with pay-per-search options in STN Express, STN Easy and STN on the Web. STN Anavist is a competitive intelligence tool to track and visualize information from patents and commercial research. The STN network is jointly operated by CAS (USA), FIZ Karlsruhe (Germany), and JAICI (Japan). A complete list of databases within STN is available online. STN includes many other scientific and technical databases as well as the databases included on Scifinder Scholar.

CAS, *STN Database Summary Sheets*, www.cas.org/support/stngen/dbss/index.html (accessed March 22, 2012).

Print *Chemical Abstracts*

The print *Chemical Abstracts* is still a useful tool for searching the historical literature. There are many guides to the print indexes. While many libraries have moved volumes to storage, a selector may need to assess the print indexes or determine if the volumes need to be weeded. This section describes the organization of the print indexes and additional tools for *Chemical Abstracts*. Effective January 1, 2010, print copies of *Chemical Abstracts* are no longer published.

CAS, *The Sections of Chemical Abstracts*, www.cas.org/products/print/ca/casections.html (accessed March 22, 2012).

CA Abstracts provides information on weekly print issues of Chemical Abstracts, including indexing and organization of content.

CAS, CA *Collective Index Content*, www.cas.org/ASSETS/B83F901AB97B493D873FCA0E194BA1F7/collectiveindexes chart.pdf (accessed March 22, 2012).

Collective Index Content shows the coverage of each collective index. The last Collective Index, the fifteenth, covered 2002–2006.

CAS, *CAS Source Index*, http://cassi.cas.org/ (accessed March 22, 2012).

The CAS Source Index, CASSI, provides an alphabetical listing (by source title abbreviation) of complete bibliographic information for all publications cited in Chemical Abstracts. Listings of libraries that own holdings of publications are also included. CASSI was formerly available in print, but is currently available on CD only.

Online Beilstein and Gmelin Handbooks

The print Beilstein handbook is currently available online through the web database Reaxsys. Online access to this handbook has gone through several previous names and searching platforms. Originally available through a client interface known as Beilstein Crossfire, the database was acquired by MDL and renamed MDL Crossfire and MDL Beilstein Crossfire. MDL was acquired by Symyx technologies in 2007 and Crossfire was distributed through them. In 2009 Rexsys was launched by Elsevier as the next-generation web tool for Beilstein Crossfire. As a new selector you may need to educate users about these name and platform changes or update information on previous client and Internet versions on the library web site.

Elsevier, *Overview|Reaxsys*, www.info.reaxys.com/about_overview (accessed March 22, 2012).

This web page has general information about coverage, searching op-tions, and features in Reaxsys. Reaxsys covers organic, inorganic and organometallic reactions, chemical properties, and data. This database complements Scifinder Scholar and provides greater historical coverage on the reaction literature. Reaxsys uses the Marvin structure editor, which is described in more detail later this chapter.

WolfWikis, MDL Crossfire Commander, http://wikis.lib.ncsu.edu/index.php/MDL_Crossfire_Commander (accessed March 22, 2012).

Archived information on the databases and functionality contained in MDL Crossfire Commander, the predecessor to Reaxys. The Crossfire Commander platform was discontinued on December 31, 2010 and is no longer active on the Elsevier web site.

Additional Chemistry Literature and Searching Interfaces

Chemspider – Database of Chemical Structures and Property Predictions, www.chemspider.com/ (accessed March 22, 2012).

Chemspider is a chemistry search engine site containing structure, property data, and synthetic procedures information for chemical substances, reactions, and property data. Information is collected from web, journal, chemical catalogs, and other sources. Chemspider is a community-based project with chemists and scientists contributing their own data, reactions, and synthetic procedures to create a free search interface. Searching is available by structure, name, and other identifiers.

Cambridge Crystallographic Data Centre, *Cambridge Structural Database (CSD)*, www.ccdc.cam.ac.uk/products/csd/ (accessed March 22, 2012).

The Cambridge Structural Database records bibliographic, chemical and crystallographic information for organic and organometallic chemical substances. More than 400,000 three-dimensional crystal structures are available. Crystal structure information is donated by scientists throughout the world. This database may be licensed through the library or directly through the chemistry department or a research lab.

Carleton College Science Education Resource Center, *Crystal Structure Databases*, http://serc.carleton.edu/research_education/crystallography/xldatabases.html (accessed March 22, 2012).

This list of crystal structure databases includes a variety of subscription as well as freely available resources.

Related Science Literature Indexes

Institution of Engineering and Technology, *INSPEC–The IET*, www.theiet.org/publishing/inspec/ (accessed March 22, 2012).

INSPEC covers nanotechnology, materials science, and chemical physics with unique coverage of materials science and engineering conference proceedings abstracts.

Engineering Information, *Compendex and EI Backfile*, www.ei.org/compendex (accessed March 22, 2012).

The online version of the print Engineering Index, this index contains more than ten million records in engineering. As with INSPEC, this source is most useful for engineering and materials applications in chemistry, especially conference proceedings coverage.

GeoScience World, *About GEOREFS*, www.geoscienceworld.org/GeoRef/georef.dtl (accessed March 22, 2012).

Maintained by the American Geological Institute (AGI), this index contains more than 2.8 million references in all areas of geology. GeorefS is most useful for studying geochemical applications in chemistry, environmental chemistry applications, water analysis, and crystallography.

General Science Literature Indexes

Thomson Reuters, *Web of Science – Science – Thomson Reuters*, http://scientific.thomson.com/products/wos/ (accessed March 22, 2012).

Web of Science is an historical research literature database and includes journals from all areas of the sciences, social sciences, and humanities. Chemists use this for interdisciplinary research needs and for determining citation counts for research articles.

Elsevier, *Scopus–What does it cover?*, www.info.sciverse.com/scopus/scopus-in-detail/facts (accessed March 22, 2012).

This comprehensive citation database contains web sites and patents as well as peer-reviewed research literature sources. As with Web of Science, chemists are likely to tabulate citation counts and explore interdisciplinary areas with this source.

Google, *About Google Scholar*, http://scholar.google.com/intl/en/scholar/about.html (accessed March 22, 2012).

This free tool from Google provides searching for research articles in all areas. Search field options are limited, and content is incomplete since authors and publishers request that their content be added to the database.

SPECIALIZED LITERATURE FORMATS

The study and research of chemistry has necessitated the development of special literature formats to disseminate research results in academia and industry.

Patents

Patents (agreements which grant inventors exclusive rights to a process or technical idea for limited periods of time) are frequently utilized by chemists and other scientists in the course of research. Chemists in both academia and industry use the patent literature extensively and an understanding of key patent resources and interpretation aids are essential to identifying U.S. and international patents. In addition to locating issued patents, selectors may also be called upon to identify the status of a patent application. Emphasis will be placed in identifying freely available and gateway sources, as well as tutorials for users and selectors to locate patent applications and international patents.

U.S. Patent and Trademark Office, *Patent Full-Text and Full-Page Image Databases*, http://patft.uspto.gov/ (accessed March 22, 2012).

The USPTO has the most extensive freely available collection of issued U.S. patents and trademarks. The database is searchable by many fields including issued patent number, inventor or assignee, and keyword. Contains links to patent images as well as full-text of issued patents. Includes patent references. Covers patents issued from 1790 to the present.

Google, *Google Patents*, www.google.com/patents (accessed March 22, 2012).

This newer site is another freely available patent searching web site. The advanced search option provides searching by a variety of fields including assignee, inventor, patent number, issue date, and filing date. Display of results includes full-text of patent including figures, as well as patent references and later patents that cite the item. Covers patents issued from 1790 to the present.

Cambia, *Patent Lens Home*, www.patentlens.net/daisy/patentlens/patentlens.html (accessed March 22, 2012).

Cambia Patent Lens is an international freely available patent database, with more than eight million patent records from the U.S. (USPTO), Europe (EPO), and Australia (IP Australia) and WIPO (World Intellectual Property Information). Searchable by keyword, assignee/inventor, and patent number, as well as additional search fields. Contains patent references, application filing status and legal information. Covers patents from 1790 to the present.

STN International, *STN International: STN Brochures: Patent Information*, www.stn-international.com/stnbrochures_pi.html (accessed March 22, 2012).

This web page from STN gives an overview of patent databases in STN, searching and display options, as well as searching examples. STN offers pay-per-search access to many patent databases, including extensive coverage of international patents and status information on patent applications.

University of Texas at Austin, *Guide to Patent Searching – University of Texas at Austin*, www.lib.utexas.edu/engin/patent-tutorial/index.htm (accessed March 22, 2012).

This online tutorial provides an excellent overview for searching the patent literature including search strategies and examples.

TECHNICAL REPORTS

Technical reports are frequently published by chemists and other scientists performing research in non-profit and commercial environments. The national laboratories in the U.S. and other countries publish reports as well as journal articles on their current research projects. Smaller research institutes, government agencies, and commercial companies may publish reports as well.

Technical reports frequently contain information not available in the journal literature and as a result can be difficult to obtain. Locating technical reports and adding them to collections for library users can be a challenge. Print runs of reports are small and often kept by scientists and researchers in their labs and offices. Few copies of technical reports are cataloged and added to collective library catalogs such as WorldCat. Costs for technical reports tend to be lower than those for books or journal issues, so price is rarely a factor in selection and budgeting.

These sources are good starting places to look for specific reports. Scientists will frequently have a reference or need for a specific technical report, with a report number or other unique identifier to locate the item. Acronyms are also common in technical report titles or number codes. A little research may be required to identify the acronyms. In addition to databases, the libraries of the U.S. national laboratories are also excellent sources to locate technical reports, especially if they were published by the lab in question. Traditional literature indexes such as EI Compendix, INSPEC, and Web of Science are also useful for searching technical reports, although that content is geared towards peer-reviewed literature.

Office of Scientific and Technical Information (OSTI), By Lab, Major Site, or Technology Center, www.osti.gov/stip/doelabs (accessed March 22, 2012).

Lists all major national labs and research centers in the U.S. with web links and acronyms.

National Technical Information Service, *NTIS-National Technical Information Service*, www.ntis.gov/ (accessed March 22, 2012).

NTIS is the largest technical report database with information on many technical reports generated by government agencies since 1964. Individual search results can be ordered through NTIS in different formats (print, CD-ROM, downloadable file, microfiche).

Google, *Google Scholar*, http://scholar.google.com/ (accessed March 22, 2012).

Google Scholar allows searching for technical reports from a variety of sources. Government as well as commercial sources are represented. Coverage is less comprehensive than NTIS and other governmental search sites.

Kathleen Gust, Stanford University Libraries, *SULAIR: How do I Find?: Technical Reports*, http://library.stanford.edu/collect/techrpt.html (accessed March 22, 2012).

This excellent guide describes and lists many additional free and fee-based sites for searching technical reports.

PREPRINTS AND PREPRINT SERVERS

The use of preprints and preprint servers in chemistry has recently evolved, and the number of resources continues to grow with the ongoing trends in scholarly publishing and information sharing. While these sites are more popular with other areas of the sciences and mathematics, academic chemistry researchers in some research areas are active preprint depositors and sharers.

Cornell University Libraries, arXiv.org, http://arxiv.org/ (accessed March 22, 2012).

arXiv is a fully automated electronic archive and distribution server for research papers in many areas of physics and the physical sciences. Begun in 1991 at Los Alamos National Laboratory (LANL) by Paul Ginsparg, it is currently housed at Cornell University Libraries and contains more than 600,000 items. A mirror site is also available at http://xxx.lanl.gov/.

Brown University, *Chemical Physics Preprint Database*, www.chem.brown.edu/chem-ph.html (accessed March 22, 2012).

Contains links to current and archived preprints in chemical physics and theoretical chemistry research.

Elsevier, Preprint Archive, www.sciencedirect.com/preprintarchive (accessed March 22, 2012).

An archive of chemistry, mathematics and computer science research preprints and experimental data. Coverage ends at 2004 and is freely available by registering on chemweb.com.

Nature, Home: Nature Precedings, http://precedings.nature.com/ (accessed March 22, 2012).

Contains preprints in all areas of the sciences, with a separate section for chemistry. Post prints, preprint manuscripts, posters, and presentations are included.

Office of Scientific and Technical Information, E-print Network Home Page – Energy, Science and Technology for the research community, www.osti.gov/eprints/ (accessed March 22, 2012).

The Department of Energy's (DOE) E-print Network, formerly the PrePRINT Network, is a searchable gateway to scientific and technical preprint servers. Searching is available for more than twenty-seven thousand preprint servers and web sites.

REPRESENTING INFORMATION

Scientists have been representing information and results visually through a variety of methods. Some visual information, such as chemical structures, evolved as a way to communicate information and represent chemical information quickly to peers. Some of the most common means of communicating are summarized here. They include naming (nomenclature) of chemicals, representing substances with stick and line structures or structure-based searching, and identifying chemicals using techniques in spectroscopy and other instruments. Additional ways of communicating information, such as mathematical equations, are omitted here, as they are not as essential to searching the literature and identifying chemical substances.

NAMING AND NOMENCLATURE OF CHEMICALS

Identifying the name of a chemical substance in the literature can be very challenging, even for selectors with a chemistry background. Chemists use the IUPAC, or International Union of Pure and Applied Chemistry, system of nomenclature to create standardized names for substances. Unfortunately, while these names are officially recognized, common and trade names for many chemicals are still used, often more frequently than the IUPAC names, because for many substances the IUPAC name is much more complex than the common name. In addition, there can be multiple common, trade, or brand names for chemicals that have evolved over time.

A variety of sources exist to assist users and selectors in locating both common and IUPAC names for chemical substances. A mixture of free and fee-based sources are available.

CAS, *CAS REGISTRY – the gold standard for substance information*, www.cas.org/expertise/cascontent/registry/index.html (accessed March 22, 2012).

Each registry entry in Scifinder Scholar contains all forms of the name used for a chemical substance, as well as the CAS registry number for the substance. Multiple common and trade names and trade names are listed alphabetically.

Sigma-Aldrich, *Sigma-Aldrich Chem Product Central*, www.sigmaaldrich.com/chemistry/chemical-synthesis/chemical-synthesis-catalog.html (accessed March 22, 2012).

The annual Sigma-Aldrich chemical catalogs are the most comprehensive commercial sources of chemicals, and are freely available in print and electronic formats. Sigma has traditionally focused on inorganic substances, and Aldrich specializes in organic chemicals. Chemical catalogs contain cross-references for common names, trade names, and IUPAC names for many common chemicals. In addition to containing name cross-references, additional data on chemical properties, chemical spectra, and chemical literature references are available for many substances.

International Union of Pure and Applied Chemistry (IUPAC), *IUPAC Gold Book*, http://goldbook.iupac.org/ (accessed March 22, 2012).

Contains naming information and guidance on all types of chemical substances. *The Gold Book* is freely available on the web. A CD-ROM version is also available. IUPAC also publishes regular volume updates on chemical nomenclature rules which can be ordered as individual volumes.

CHEMICAL STRUCTURE SEARCHING

Chemists frequently use chemical structures, or line drawings of chemical substances with chemical symbols noted, as shorthand for describing their research. Chemical structures can be difficult to draw, and the chemical literature has been developed to facilitate identification of substances by incorporating chemical structure search capabilities into existing databases. In any chemical literature research tool, this feature is one of the most powerful for the chemist to quickly identify and predict chemical behavior for unknown substances. All of the literature databases for chemistry contain some type of structure drawing software which can be incorporated into searches. This section will focus on sources to guide a new selector in learning to use these tools effectively for patrons.

CambridgeSoft, CambridgeSoft Desktop Software–ChemDraw, www.cambridgesoft.com/software/details/?ds=2 (accessed March 22, 2012).

Chemdraw is the chemical drawing software tool used most frequently by practicing chemists and scientists for technical writing and manuscript preparation. Individual and site licenses are available. In large academic and corporate settings this license may be available to all employees. In smaller organizations, access to the site license may be limited. New selectors should check with a representative from their research labs or academic department to determine the level of access available.

Chang Bioscience, *Chemical Structure Drawing*, www.changbioscience.com/mis/chemdraw.html (accessed March 22, 2012).

Java Molecular Editor (JME) is freely available software containing basic structure drawing features.

Chem Axon, Marvin-ChemAxon – toolkits and desktop applications for cheminformatics, www.chemaxon.com/products/marvin/ (accessed March 22, 2012).

Marvin is a suite of products to visualize and process chemical information. Marvin Sketch is a chemical structure drawing tool and editor; other products include MarvinSpace, MarvinView, and MolConvertor, which perform more advanced structure manipulation and analysis. Desktop versions of the Marvin family are freely available.

Accelrys, AccelrysDraw, http://accelrys.com/products/informatics/cheminformatics/draw/ (accessed March 22, 2012).

Accelrys provides a free version of Accelrys Draw for academic use. This tool was formerly called Symyx Draw from Symyx, and IsisDraw from MDL Labs.

SPECTROSCOPIC INFORMATION

The study of the interaction between radiation and matter, or spectroscopy, is an essential tool that chemists use for several purposes: to observe how substances behave at certain energy levels, to identify a chemical substance, and to predict behavior of unknown substances or newly synthesized materials from ones already characterized. Spectra are collected and made available through journal articles, reference sources, and collections of individual spectra.

There are several types of spectroscopy chemists encounter frequently in research. Electromagnetic spectroscopy concerns interactions with electromagnetic radiation or light. Examples include ultraviolet (UV), visible and, infra-red (IR) spectra. Mass spectroscopy or mass spectrometry covers the interaction of charged species with a magnetic field. The resulting interaction results in a mass spectrum. Nuclear Magnetic Resonance (NMR) uses magnets to spin electrons and measures detailed chemical structure elements and functional groups. Identification sources for each type of spectroscopy are profiled with freely available sources noted.

Internetchemie, *Spectroscopy*, www.internetchemistry.com/chemistry/spectroscopy.htm (accessed March 22, 2012).

This site gives useful background information on spectroscopy and defines useful terminology and concepts. All areas of spectroscopy theory and practice are covered.

BioRad, *KnowItAll University Academic Edition Web Site*, www.knowitall.com/academic/welcome.asp (accessed March 22, 2012).

Bio-Rad KnowItAll University Online Spectra Database, which replaced the Sadtler spectra series in green binder volumes, contains a variety of IR spectra types including Standard Infrared, IR Grating Spectra, Standard Grating Spectra, Standard IR Grating Spectra, IR Prism Spectra, and Standard Infrared Vapor Phase Spectra. Use of this source is more limited now that more finely resolved IR data (Fourier-Transform Infrared, or FT-IR) is the standard in laboratory practice. Standard Ultraviolet Spectra are included as well Standard Carbon-13 NMR Spectra and Standard NMR Spectra.

Charles J. Pouchert, *The Aldrich Library of Infrared Spectra* (Milwaukee, Wis.: Aldrich Chemical Co., 1981).

Charles Pouchert, *The Aldrich Library of FT-IR Spectra*, 2nd. ed. (New York: Wiley, 1997).

Charles J. Pouchert, *The Aldrich Library of NMR Spectra*, 2nd. ed. (Milwaukee, Wis.: Aldrich Chemical Co., 1983).

Charles J. Pouchert, *The Aldrich Library of 13C and 1H FT NMR Spectra* (Milwaukee, Wis.: Aldrich Chemical Co., 1993).

This Aldrich spectra volume series contains print volumes for IR and NMR spectra. This essential reference source contains a number of chemical spectra. Also available on CD-ROM. This is an essential reference collection title for chemistry and is heavily used.

Fiveash Data Management, *FDM Library Search Tutorial*, www.fdmspectra.com/FDM_Library_Search_Tutorial.htm (accessed March 22, 2012).

FDM is an online subscription source for IR spectra for several types of chemical substances including polymers and polymer additives, surfactants, organic compounds, and minerals and inorganic compounds.

National Institute of Standards and Technology, *Welcome to the NIST Chemistry Web Book*, http://webbook.nist.gov/ (accessed March 22, 2012).

The NIST Chemistry web book is a freely accessible online source for online IR spectra and contains more than 5,000 FT-IR, UV, and NMR spectra.

National Institute of Advanced Industrial Science and Technology (AIST), *AIST: RIO-DB Spectral Database for Organic Compounds — SDBS*, http://riodb01.ibase.aist.go.jp/sdbs/cgi-bin/cre_index.cgi?lang=eng (accessed March 22, 2012).

SDBS is a freely available web resource from Japan with IR, NMR and Mass spectral data.

Advanced Chemistry Development (ACD) Labs, *Analytical Data Handling*, www.acdlabs.com/products/adh/ (accessed March 22, 2012).

ACD has several subscription databases with IR, UV, NMR, and mass spectral curated data.

NMR ShiftDB, *NMR ShiftDB – open nmr database on the web*, www.nmrshiftdb.org/ (accessed March 22, 2012).

NMRShiftDB is a community-based, open, freely available NMR spectra database where scientists submit spectra for substances. More than 45,000 spectra are available.

Angela J. Brandolini and Deborah D. Hills, *NMR Spectra of Polymers and Polymer Additives* (New York: Marcel Dekker, 2000).

Herman A. Szymanski, *Infrared Band Handbook*, 2nd ed. (New York: IFI/Plenum, 1970).

G. Socrates, *Infrared and Raman Characteristic Group Frequencies*, 3rd ed. (Chichester ; New York : Wiley, 2001).

David Dolphin, *Tabulation of Infrared Spectral Data* (New York: Wiley, 1977).

University of California, Los Angeles, *IR Absorption Table*, www.chem.ucla.edu/~webspectra/irtable.html (accessed March 22, 2012).

These titles and web site contain print volumes with IR spectra and aids for interpreting spectral data. These titles are useful as print reference sources.

University of Arizona Department of Chemistry, Mass Spectrometry Tutorial, www.chem.arizona.edu/massspec/ (accessed March 22, 2012).

Online tutorial that explains mass spectral data features and gives an overview of spectra interpretation.

LABORATORY PRACTICE IN CHEMISTRY

Since chemists are frequently in the lab and work with many different types of chemicals, the need for current and accurate safety information on these substances, as well information on how to purchase chemicals from commercial sources, is essential. This section concentrates on freely available and comprehensive sites for all types of selectors. Selectors in specialized chemical environments will also have access to additional pay-per-search and commercial sources.

CHEMICAL SAFETY DATA

The standard format for listing chemical safety information is a Material Safety Data Sheet (MSDS), for an individual chemical. The MSDS contains important safety information such as:

- chemical flammability
- carcinogenic properties
- explosiveness and stability of the substance
- the temperature range at which a chemical should be stored
- the potential to release lethal fumes
- complications from exposure to skin or soft tissue

• precautions in dispensing or disposing of the chemical
• potential fatal complications from using the substance

MSDS are regulated by law and are listed in a number of free and commercial sources in the link below. Chemical supply catalogs are also useful in providing MSDS information and helping to locate MSDS information for commercially available chemicals. Local collections may also have a set of MSDS sheets on file or bound collections of MSDS information. Make sure this information is current when assessing the collection.

Interactive Learning Paradigms, Incorporated, *Where to find MSDS on the Internet*, www.ilpi.com/msds/index.html (accessed March 22, 2012).

This web site provides a comprehensive listing of online sources for Material Safety Data Sheet information. Information is grouped by commercial and non-profit sites and includes the number of MSDS records and comments for each site.

LOCATING COMMERCIAL CHEMICALS

Chemists frequently need to identify and purchase commercially available chemicals, meaning those which are produced in large (and small) quantities for purchase by individuals and organizations. The number of producers of chemicals is huge; in addition to large chemical companies, there are many specialty chemical suppliers. Many of these suppliers can be difficult to locate.

This section lists comprehensive online and print sources for chemical substances. Many of these sources are freely available. Performing advanced searches on web search engines can also be used to identify commercial chemicals online. Frequently, however, these results are incomplete or may not provide adequate information on details of the chemical substance.

eMolecules, *eMolecules.com|Chemical Structure Drawing Search*, www.emolecules.com/index.php (accessed March 22, 2012).

eMolecules is a free source for locating commercial chemicals by structure and keyword searching.

CAS, *CHEMCATS, Commercially Available Chemicals*, www.cas.org/expertise/cascontent/chemcats.html (accessed March 22, 2012).

CHEMCATS includes information on common and specialty commercially available chemicals. It links with the substance and reaction databases REGISTRY and CASREACT on Scifinder Scholar and by pay-per-search through STN.

ThomasNet, *ThomasNet – Browse Categories > Chemicals*, www.thomasnet.com (accessed March 22, 2012).

ThomasNet is the free online version of the print *Thomas Register*, a comprehensive directory of commercial suppliers of goods. Searching is available by trade or brand name or browsing by class of chemical.

CHEMICAL PROPERTIES AND DATA

Locating chemical properties and specific data on chemical reactions is frequently required for research in chemistry and other scientific disciplines. The scope of chemical properties is vast, with frequent use of special nomenclature, terminology, and symbols. Navigating and selecting appropriate materials to best help chemists and other patrons successfully locate the data they require can be difficult. Luckily, there are key print titles and web sites that can be used to locate information. In addition to collections of data, the chemical research literature frequently provides data and analysis of chemical properties and can be used to locate individual chemical property data. As these searches are frequently more time-consuming than searching print and online reference volumes, they should be considered after the reference sources have been consulted. Scifinder Scholar, Reaxsys and Chemspider are also rich sources of chemical property data.

The selected sources below are key reference tools for any chemistry collection, and the web site links contain additional property sources in both print and electronic formats. While databases can help in locating information, online search interfaces differ in scope and depth of indexing fields. Many print sources can still be the quickest way to locate data for library users.

CRC, *Handbook of Chemistry and Physics*, www.hbcpnetbase.com/ (accessed March 22, 2012).

The oldest and most comprehensive one-volume property handbook, commonly known as the CRC Handbook. Updated annually, it provides comprehensive property information for organic and inorganic chemical compounds. Access is available online through the CRCNetBase platform.

James Speight, *Lange's Handbook of Chemistry 70th Anniversary Edition*, 16th. ed. (New York: McGraw Hill Professional, 2004).

Considered an essential reference source for chemical property searching, this one-volume handbook contains data on many commonly used chemical properties. This title is often referred to as Lange's Handbook. The scope is less comprehensive than the CRC Handbook and is published less frequently. It is available online from Knovel as an e-book.

Maryadele J. O'Neil, *The Merck Index: An Encyclopedia of Chemicals, Drugs, and Biologicals*, 14th ed. (Whitehouse Station, N.J.: Merck, 2006).

The Merck Index is considered one of the premier sources for locating chemical property data and safety information for commonly used chemicals, drugs, and biological chemicals. Provides cross-references for common chemical names and trade names. This index is useful for locating safety data for chemicals and toxicity information, and is available online through CambridgeSoft and searchable in DIALOG and STN databases.

Anne Langley, Duke University, *Index of property names*, http://library.duke.edu/research/subject/guides/chemical-physical-properties/ (accessed March 22, 2012).

This comprehensive guide lists print sources for many different types of chemical and physical properties. Call numbers for print titles are listed. Annotated web site information is also available. Other libraries have adapted this format for their library guides.

David Flaxbart, University of Texas at Austin, *ThermoDex*, www.lib.utexas.edu/thermodex/ (accessed March 22, 2012).

Online meta-database developed to search by property and chemical type. ThermoDex also provides descriptions and links to literature sources and library call number information.

six

Chemistry Approval Plans

For many sudden selectors, it can be difficult to locate details and strategies for using approval plans to select library materials. There are few sources to consult and an in-house expert may not be available to answer questions. It can also be difficult to adapt approval plan practices from one discipline to another as chemistry has expensive individual titles. Approval practices and customs vary at different libraries, including terminology, practice and expectations for use and scope of the library collection. Collections budget size and shelf space limitations also influence collection building.

This chapter explores the process of creating, reviewing, and refining approval plans in chemistry and chemical technology. It will progress from general considerations on determining the feasibility of an approval plan to creating a new plan, reviewing and refining an existing profile, and analyzing collections data to maximize effectiveness of the plan.

WHAT ARE APPROVAL PLANS?

An approval plan is a profile or account created by a vendor to send volumes of materials to a library in a systematic and specific way. The plan can include print and online materials such as e-books, multimedia, and mixed media. In some institutions one profile is created for all subject areas, with exceptions and special directions for some parts of the profile. Other libraries create separate profiles for each subject area or academic department represented. The organization and structure of an approval plan can vary by vendor, with some plans based on LC subject headings, LC or Dewey call numbers, or locally created subject headings. Approval plans can cover titles directly shipped to the library as well as notifications for new titles sent as electronic alerts.

Approval plans in chemistry are created to monitor the major work produced through prominent U.S. and international publishers and professional societies. Academic, non-profit, and corporate institutions utilize approval plans to ensure teaching, research, and basic information needs and projects are adequately supported. Academic libraries frequently utilize approval plans, usually through multiple vendors and profiles. Corporate, museum, and non-profit libraries tend to be less frequent users of chemistry approval plans, with a narrower focus and emphasis on specialized titles relevant to the organization's research focus. Public libraries utilize approval plans to collect general interest chemistry titles and possibly study aids and guides or local interest materials.

WHY ARE APPROVAL PLANS HELPFUL?

For a selector, approval plans provide a systematic way to monitor publishing output in a discipline. It eliminates the need to pore through print and online publisher catalogs for new titles, check for new editions of popular works, or take the time to read reviews of titles to determine the audience level and suitability for your collection. The vendor also provides a price discount on selected titles, an important benefit of the plan. It can also commit an organization to purchase a significant number of titles annually. Approval plans also provide access to knowledgeable sales agents and bibliographers, which can save significant amounts of time in collection management. Usually the sales agent has an in-depth knowledge of publishing trends and output in all subject areas. The agent can also provide updates and training on generating collections data from purchases as well as rejected titles.

Most major approval plan vendors comprehensively cover chemistry and related disciplines. Commercial scientific publishers and major university presses in the U.S. and Western Europe are well-represented. Non-English and non-Western materials (except for German materials covered by foreign language vendors), as well as university press titles from smaller countries, can be more difficult to comprehensively cover through approval plans. As of this writing, the YBP approval plan structure offers the most specificity and detail and will be used as the model for later discussion.

Before establishing a new approval plan, some considerations are necessary. These include, but are not limited to, expected staff time savings from the plan, the number of individual requests from patrons, staffing levels and space for approval staging and review, and the speed with which collections are expected to change. Any of these factors might make it difficult to implement and sustain an approval plan.

APPROVAL PLAN VENDORS

Major U.S. approval plan vendors comprehensively cover chemistry and chemical technology from major commercial scientific publishers and university presses based in the U.S. and Western Europe. Major foreign approval plan vendors for chemistry specialize in Continental Europe and German language materials. German and some Japanese materials are frequently covered by foreign language vendors. Non-English and non-Western materials and some international university presses can be difficult to comprehensively cover through approval plans. Regional approval plan vendors can provide excellent coverage for smaller collections. They can frequently be located through exhibitor listings for state and regional library conferences or sponsorship lists for local library meetings.

Baker & Taylor YBP Library Services, *YBP.com – Approval Plans*, www.ybp.com/approval_plans.html (accessed March 22, 2012).

Originated in 1971 and originally called Yankee Book Peddler, services include approval plans, a book awards program that ships major literary award-winning titles, consortial support, a continuations program, deposit account programs, e-book and e-reference work support, firm order placement, ILS integration, and a key reviews service that ships titles from major sources such as *Nature* and *Science*. The online support database GOBI (Global Online Bibliographic Information) contains more than 2 million English-language titles for online queries, selection, ordering, approval plan notifications, and data reporting. Divisions of YBP include Blackwell U.K., supplier of UK and Continental Europe titles, J.A. Majors, which specializes in medical titles, and Baker & Taylor, which handles book distribution. YBP offers approval plan profiles based on LC call numbers and non-subject parameters.

Coutts Library Services, *Coutts–delivering to libraries worldwide*, www.couttsinfo.com/Services/services.htm (accessed March 22, 2012).

Coutts Information Services, begun in 1969, offers many collections services including approval plans, e-book support, new title notifications, out-of-print titles, and shelf-ready book services for U.S., Canadian, and U.K. libraries. The online selection and ordering database OASIS (Online Acquisition and Selection Information System) contains more than 5 million titles from standing orders, approval, and firm orders. This system has many of the features of the other major approval plan vendors. Coutts emphasizes the strength of its e-book online ordering and support.

Harrassowitz, *Monographs*, www.harrassowitz.de/book_services/monographs.html (accessed March 22, 2012).

Harrassowitz, begun in 1872 as an antiquarian bookseller, offers a variety of subscription and book services including approval plans, e-book support, and new title announcements. Continental Europe and German language materials are covered through the online database OttoEditions, which contains more than two million titles and music scores. Harrassowitz is a useful vendor to consider if a collection has a large number of German-language titles, is a German-owned organization or has a large number of German-language programs or an extensive translation program.

Some criteria to consider when selecting or reviewing approval plan vendors include the expertise of the sales agent and bibliographers on the staff, the ability to monitor and report on plan activity with reports and status updates, prompt shipping and timely service, the level of detail and specificity available in a plan, the ability to quickly adjust and implement profile changes, a large inventory available to select and ship, and ability to incorporate multidisciplinary areas and foreign language materials easily into the plan profile.

PUBLISHER LISTS

Publisher lists are an effective way to guide selection and refine approval plans in a discipline. Approval plan vendors frequently publish a variety of publisher and title lists to support collection development and acquisition of new materials. Each vendor will have reports and additional information to help guide selectors.

Lists of most popular titles and essential titles are the most useful for a new selector or those with limited funds. These provide a way to screen for recently published popular titles. Many specialized titles may not be on these lists, as they are frequently skewed to more popular titles targeted to lower-level audiences.

Examples of the types of publisher lists available include complete publisher lists, which are less useful for a new selector in a specific discipline; core publisher lists, which are useful when there are limited funds or smaller profiles; subject-specific publisher lists, which are the most useful for a new selector.

Baker & Taylor YBP Library Services, *Subject Specific Publisher Lists: Science and Technology*, www.ybp.com/PublisherLists/science.pdf (accessed March 22, 2012).

REVIEWING EXISTING APPROVAL PLANS

It may be difficult to determine when an approval plan profile was last updated. When collections liaison roles have been vacant for long periods, profiles can be neglected, so assume that the profile has been static since the last full-time identified selector was present. A vendor representative for the plan can also help determine a profile's past activity.

Chemistry is covered in the Library of Congress classification scheme in call number ranges QD (Chemistry) and TP (Chemical Technology). Additional call number ranges that can cover interdisciplinary research areas in chemistry include QP501–981 (Physiology), TA401–492 (Materials Science) and TD1–1066 (Environmental Technology). The Dewey Decimal classification area for chemistry is 540–549 (Chemistry & Allied Sciences).

Chemistry collections tend to have a smaller number of titles published at all levels: juvenile, popular, general academic, and professional. Popular titles are less frequent and limited to biographies, general information, and guides. Many undergraduate and graduate textbooks in chemistry are published annually, most with supplemental solution and instructor guides. Professional-level specialized texts are frequently published and specialized multivolume book series are also popular. Festschriften, which are collections of tribute essays and sometimes previously published material, and conference proceedings are infrequently published. Do not worry about comprehensively covering narrower subject headings when initially reviewing a profile. In some cases these areas are not represented well in the literature and will have little effect on profile activity.

REVIEWING NONSUBJECT PARAMETERS

For the purposes of this discussion YBP Library Services subject parameters will be discussed. Some non-subject plan parameters will require special attention and will be covered individually in this section, including format, language, content level, new editions, non-book formats, place of publication, price ceilings, reference books, sets and series, and translations.

Formats that may require special attention include biographies, collected works, conference monographs and proceedings, festschriften, instructor and lab manuals, personal narratives, revised dissertations, study guides, and textbooks. In most cases, these materials can be limited to notifications rather than approval books to conserve funds. Chemists rarely consult conference proceedings, festschriften, and collected works. Lab manuals and study guides can also be limited in approval plans. Frequently, faculty and instructors receive these as review texts for courses. It is best to check and see if they have been placed on reserve prior to adding them to the collection, as some instructors use content in these guides for problem sets and test questions. They are also frequently donated as gifts. Check to make sure any copies selected to be added to the collection are not considered prepublication review copies, which may have a disclaimer that the text cannot be resold. Revised and unrevised dissertations are infrequently requested, and can also be ordered cheaply as reprints through sources such as UMI. Textbooks can also be omitted in approval plans, as the selector can rely on faculty reserve requests for titles to complete this area of the collection. One exception to textbooks is classic graduate and professional textbooks, which are highly used in many academic collections; in these cases multiple copies may be obtained through donations or gifts.

Language coverage in approval plans is usually limited to English language only unless there is a need for coverage in a specialized area. Language translation materials such as foreign language dictionaries and research aids can be useful for larger collections. If your institution has a translation program it may be helpful to include selected foreign language titles.

Content levels of materials in chemistry usually require some consideration. Juvenile content is frequently limited to public library collections. Popular materials can be of use to all types of libraries, depending on the scope and coverage of material. General and advanced academic materials are necessary for academic collections, and professional level content will usually be found in larger academic collections and specialized technical libraries. As a general rule, the larger the funds, the more advanced academic and professional titles should be ordered. These titles can be matched to faculty member research interests by looking at faculty member profiles.

New editions of works are frequently published in chemistry, and special attention should be paid to the quality and extent of revisions in new and updated editions of texts. Usually book reviews and book advertisements give insight into the scope of these changes to determine if purchase of a new edition is necessary. Critical editions, supplements, and abridged titles are infrequently published and there will be little need for them.

Several non-book formats may require additional attention in approval plans. Some texts include CD-ROMs or supplemental material that may require additional processing. Audio and video materials will likely be best limited to public library or specialized technical libraries, unless requested as a special course tool or reserves supplement. Some books may contain links or password access to online content, usually limited to textbooks. This should not be a primary factor in selection.

Place of publication can be one criterion to consider carefully. If the approval plan includes titles published from multiple countries, unless there is a compelling reason to limit funds it is better to receive notification from all of the countries and publishing environments. In this way it is easier to monitor titles published under multiple imprints and eliminate duplication in ordering. Many approval plans allow customers to select the preferred version to receive as a notification or the book itself. It is recommended that the U.S. version be purchased when possible. In most cases the U.S. version will be the first version and the one of record.

Price ceilings for chemistry books will need to be set at higher levels than for other disciplines. Single volume price limits of between $250 and $300 and multivolume limits of $500 ensure that the majority of titles come through the profile and the more expensive items are moved to notifications. When in doubt, add an extra $50 to $100 for book title limits to make sure essential titles arrive through the plan.

Reprints are becoming less common in chemistry but are occasionally published. Many approval plan vendors note previously published material in their notification plans. For most plans it is best to eliminate reprints, facsimiles, and journal monograph items in the profile. These are frequently money-makers for publishers and provide no new content or perspective.

Reference books in chemistry approval plans are usually limited to almanacs, bibliographies, biographical dictionaries, dictionaries, directories, encyclopedias, and handbooks. Other reference formats are rarely published and can be excluded from the profile. As the output of reference titles in chemistry is small but the cost per item is large (large reference sets in chemistry are frequently more than $3,000) it is best to receive reference title notifications rather than the approval copies of the materials. Reference e-books are standard in chemistry. It is recommended that reference titles be purchased in this format when possible. Many libraries have stopped purchasing large, comprehensive reference sets in chemistry, especially in print, due to low use. If reference funds are strained, consider limiting purchases to titles costing from $150 to $175 or less. There should be quality titles in this price range (even as e-books) that will cover patrons' core reference needs.

Sets and series are an important non-subject parameter in chemistry, with many sets published in all areas of the discipline. Usually these are specialized volumes targeted to specific research needs. For any large or comprehensive collection, notifications should be set up for all numbered series, unnumbered series, initial volumes of new series, and lecture series. Series titles can also be easily switched from notifications to book shipments if necessary. Comprehensive series are extremely expensive ($5,000 and up). It is recommended that the selector check and see if a previous edition of the set is already in the collection, if the set is available as an e-book, or if the title has been requested by a patron. If so, then it may be worthwhile to purchase the set.

Translations of titles in chemistry are infrequent but should still be set up as a part of a notification plan. As expected, translations into English will be much more commonplace than translations from English.

Descriptive parameters for chemistry can include pictorial works, practical guidebooks, titles on the teaching of chemistry, and vocational/technician guides. Depending on the size and scope of the collection, these parameters are important to ensure non-chemists' needs are covered. Enabling notification is the easiest way to monitor this output.

SWITCHING BACK AND FORTH BETWEEN NOTIFICATIONS AND SHIPPED TITLES

Approval notifications are useful to quickly monitor publishing output without committing funds. As a new selector, it can be difficult to determine how broad to set a notification plan. Since the publishing output in chemistry is relatively smaller than many disciplines, it is recommended to set the notification profile to include most new titles. Over time it becomes easier to limit call number ranges and non-subject parameters in the profile. It is recommended that either non-subject parameters or call numbers be adjusted to best gauge the effects on profile activity. Criteria to consider with notification profiles are summarized and include publisher prestige, potential circulation, and vendor profile reports.

While publisher prestige in chemistry is subjective, many scientists and librarians consider major scientific and scholarly societies as the most prestigious. Multiple book reviews by major publications is one sign of an essential title. The intended level of the audience is another indicator. Specialized titles can be collected more selectively, especially titles identified as such by plan vendors. As a general rule, titles from core publishers should be sent as direct shipments and less prominent publishers monitored as approval notifications. These publishers will be similar for all areas of the sciences. Looking at another science profile for publisher coverage is a quick way to adjust direct shipment and notification by publisher.

Potential circulation of an item is a consideration. Many non-chemists use chemistry titles as learning and review tools. Some titles may have local authors or local interest which may raise circulation statistics. Historically significant titles are of value to non-scientists. Items requested by researchers, faculty, and students are also likely to have higher circulation activity, and represent areas which require additional collections support. Any item meeting these criteria can be monitored and moved to direct ship as needed.

Reports and statistical data from the online selection databases contain helpful guides to selection. The level of purchasing activity for an individual title is a reliable indicator of popularity and accessibility to a general audience. Locating or subscribing to collection data from peer institutions also provides a rich source of selection insight, especially if the peer institution has an experienced selector. Notes such as details on format, readership level, series title information, and book review dates are also helpful for chemistry selection and adjusting the mix of shipped vs. notification titles.

COLLECTION STATISTICS AND SELECTION

There are a variety of tools available to a selector to look at a collection's usage. While not all types of data may be helpful in seeing long-term publication and collection trends, judicious use of collections data can be valuable in determining selection priorities and adjusting approval plans.

Generating lists of titles selected by call number or subject is one way to look at collection growth. Many approval plan vendors can provide data on titles either selected and rejected. An advanced library catalog search can give a rough guide to titles selected if approval plan vendor data is not available. Data on rejected approval plan titles is also helpful in narrowing the scope of a profile or adjusting non-subject parameters.

In-house data from circulation, interlibrary loan, and reserves activity is also very helpful in analyzing trends and discovering unmet collection needs. Depending on the library circulation data available, circulation data can show what patrons are browsing and checking out. Reserves information can show which titles are heavily used for courses. In academic libraries, faculty members frequently use personal texts for reserves. Identifying these texts and adding titles is another way to acquire new materials. Heavily used textbooks may require additional copies be added to the collection. Interlibrary loan requests and items frequently sent as requested items for interlibrary loan are good candidates for extra copies of titles through gifts or purchase.

Strategies to narrow the scope of an approval plan include limiting subject and non-subject parameters. Judicious adjustment of these areas along with analysis of collection acquisition data can allow further refinement of a profile and show collection trends and unmet needs.

ANTICIPATING FUTURE COLLECTION TRENDS

Most selectors monitor and refine approval plans regularly, and these general guidelines from other disciplines apply well to chemistry. As noted earlier, the cost of materials and scope of coverage will be the primary considerations when adjusting a profile. Other considerations, such as the scope of research, patron requests, and growth of newer areas of research will also influence approval plan adjustments.

For academic and corporate libraries, getting a sense of new hires in a department or research division will help anticipate future needs. Newly established departments and disciplines frequently have unmet collection needs. Balancing these new needs with established programs can be a challenge. In a corporate setting, reading the company's annual research report can also help locate the relevant terminology about projects to best search for titles. Public libraries and smaller academic institutions can review popular science magazines and local news stories that cover chemistry and chemical topics to anticipate future collection needs.

Areas in chemistry that may need more refinement and adjustment are chemical engineering and materials science. Both disciplines have materials classed as T's in the LC classification scheme. Additional ideas to analyze selection of materials and manage collection growth will be discussed in the next chapter.

seven

General Selection Advice

Selecting and building a collection in chemistry is an ongoing process. There are always new materials to order and new web tools and new versions of indexes and online databases to consider. New publishing models and information channels for faster communication with scientists become available on a regular basis. The field of chemistry is rapidly growing to include newer interdisciplinary areas. Striking a balance between rapid growth and careful reflection with materials can be difficult. This chapter offers general advice on selection and collections planning in chemistry.

TIME MANAGEMENT STRATEGIES

Sudden selectors often find that new collections responsibilities are added to existing responsibilities and selection areas meaning that they have many disciplines to monitor, usually in addition to other activities such as reference desk service, course and library instruction, or specialized literature searches and patron consultations. Time management is essential to effectively select appropriate content for a variety of areas. Selectors tend to develop their own individual workflows and routines to effectively monitor titles and keep abreast of new developments. Keeping this in mind, general suggestions and approaches include the following.

DAILY

Updating and awareness activities. Develop a daily routine that involves any one of the sources in chapter 3, a social network, or local groups or within your discipline of study. This routine should be flexible enough to accommodate last-minute projects and also extensive enough to provide useful information. If your time is severely limited, consider aggregating blog feeds, social networking tools, and discussion list messages into folders or web sites to check when you can. Announcements regarding publishers, databases, and products are usually rapidly shared among colleagues. While learning about useful reference sources and unusual reference questions is helpful, this content will likely be of limited value in selecting new materials.

EVERY TWO TO FOUR WEEKS

Review new titles and selection lists from approval plan vendors. Looking at large batches of titles at once can save time and can give a better perspective on the scope of material published in chemistry. In the absence of an approval plan profile, browsing titles by subject from amazon.com (subjects/science/chemistry) or other online book vendors provides useful information on popular title output.

Vendor brochures are also extremely helpful in learning about new book series and updated journal costs, as well as for identifying major reference works. Keep these in a pile or e-mail folder for several months to keep track of new announcements. Visiting exhibitor booths and attending vendor activities at conferences for both librarians and scientists (such as the American Chemical Society meetings) are excellent ways to learn quickly about new developments in databases and electronic access to materials. At conferences, allow time to network with peers and talk directly to vendors about their products. Exhibitors can also show new search features and expanded coverage more quickly than online webinars and tutorials.

REGULARLY

Allocate blocks of time to select materials. Many librarians use reference desk shifts or other regularly scheduled times to select titles, and review patron requests and gifts. Dividing the annual budget allocation into monthly or weekly allotments is a good way to estimate ordering levels and ensure there are adequate funds for the remainder of the fiscal year. It is also a good idea to keep a small amount of money in reserve for the end of the ordering cycle, in case a must-have title is requested or comes in on the approval plan. Maintaining electronic or print folders for each discipline with separate files for yes/no/maybe titles can also save time with selection.

Create a tool to quickly record and monitor ordering amounts and fund activity. A paper or electronic spreadsheet with ordering amounts and fund availability information on total allocation amounts, encumbrance levels, and freely available funds saves a lot of time with selection. It also helps with planning for ordering more expensive monograph and reference sets. Listing individual titles ordered can be time-consuming. The library OPAC or acquisitions module in an integrated library system (ILS) can provide this information instead. If your organization doesn't have an ILS, consider keeping invoices from vendors to monitor fund spending.

FUND MANAGEMENT: YEARLY PLANNING AND BUDGETING

Planning selecting activities throughout the fiscal year can require adjustments, especially if a new subject area is added part-way through the fiscal year or at a busy time. The considerations that follow are intended as a general guide for different scenarios.

At what point in the fiscal year are duties to begin? If there is limited time to order materials, concentrating in ordering more popular titles and large monographic sets are ways to maximize selection of materials. It is also useful to check and see if any notes were left behind by a previous selector.

Another consideration is the annual activity in the organization and the ways funds are spent. Are receipts or other information easily available from the previous selector's activities? This is a useful way to gain insight into selecting materials. What was ordered for course reserves or other special applications and projects? These titles and areas are likely to be of interest in the future. Lost or missing item reports are also useful to determine gaps in the collection.

Publishing activity can vary within the fiscal year and from one fiscal year to the next. It is better to spend conservatively earlier in the year and keep lists of titles on hand to order later, in case there are more must-have titles published toward the end of the year. Popular science topics such as global warming, climate change, and nanotechnology are frequently over-represented in title output. Publishers do this to capitalize on interest from recent popular news events. Pay attention to this in the selection process to ensure balanced coverage.

SETTING SELECTION PRIORITIES AND CRITERIA

Determining selection priorities with limited funds can be another challenge for a new selector. In addition to the high cost of individual titles, there are other factors to consider in prioritizing purchases. Some are listed below for general guidance. Keep in mind there may be general selection criteria at your organization that will override these rules.

Requests from patrons and faculty should be high priority, as well as course reserve materials, and any items required for accreditation or certification, such as the ACS-endorsed programs in chemistry. Be prepared to provide documentation on these required tools when collections are reviewed or programs are evaluated. This guide notes the tools that are expected to be available for chemistry undergraduate and graduate programs.

Shipped approval books should generally be considered higher priority than those selected through notifications, although practice at individual institutions may vary. Consider new and revised editions of books critically. Take note of the extent of revisions and corrected or updated material. Try to limit the purchase of textbooks and other expensive tertiary literature titles, unless they are used for teaching and curriculum support. Also consider if a researcher, faculty member, or community user would request the title in question if it is not ordered immediately

Gifts and unsolicited materials should be lower priority items unless other areas of the library such as special collections or archives are interested. In many cases, gift review should occur after selection and spending activities are accomplished. Sometimes, large gifts may require additional time to analyze. Keep in mind that less information on titles and holdings may be available for these larger gifts. One quick test is to identify a sample set, say fifty to one hundred titles, and analyze them carefully for relevance, value, condition, and scope. If you see titles to add from the sample set, then the gift will require more analysis and review. Also consider if the gift is from a living donor who may contribute more materials in the future.

Cost of items is one factor in determining selection priorities. If a title costs more than $500 per set or more than $500 per volume, purchasing print material will probably not justify the cost of the item. Likewise, if a title is likely to be used for course reserves, high use of the item may justify the cost. If funds are extremely limited, make selection of general titles the highest priority, especially if they will be used by the general public.

COLLABORATING WITH PEERS AND PATRONS

Successful collaboration with professional peers and library patrons are effective ways to maintain relevant, highly used collections. Developing a list of peer institutions or organizations is an excellent way to develop a peer network, especially if this has not been done for the larger collections profile. The web social software applications described in chapter 3 such as Facebook, blogs, and professional organizations are invaluable in identifying appropriate peer institutions for reference, instruction, and selection. Your institutional mission statement and planning documents can also help provide peer information, as well as the library mission statement or strategic plan.

Developing relationships with library users can also be rewarding and lead to more effective title selection and collections growth. Communicating with library users through community, research, and teaching events are also excellent ways to connect with users and get insight into selection needs and perceptions of the library's services. Social functions and informal gatherings are also effective tools to reach library patrons.

Involvement in professional organizations such as the American Chemical Society provides an excellent outreach opportunity, especially if chemistry selection is expected to continue indefinitely or intended as a permanent assignment. Attending society meetings will provide opportunities to directly interact with chemists and identify research trends quickly as well as provide opportunities to network with other chemistry librarians.

DESELECTING AND TRANSFERRING MATERIALS

Deselecting and transferring materials is necessary in any subject, but these aspects of collection management can be problematic for a new selector. It can be difficult to decide whether to transfer an item to off-site storage or withdraw. Space constraints and deadlines also frequently force quick decisions on these matters, with little planning time. To complicate matters, many older titles in the sciences can be difficult to replace and may be needed as historical tools for other disciplines.

Fortunately, the life span of research materials in most areas of chemistry is quite short, approximately twenty years. Most books and journals more than twenty years old will be unlikely to be extensively used or required on-site in the library. Items with little or no circulation can be weeded or transferred to an off-site storage facility. If your institution has a strong program in the history of science, it is recommended that titles not be withdrawn if other shelf space is available. Titles with no circulation that have at least fifty copies within the WorldCat database can be safely withdrawn from the collection.

Transferring and weeding print journals is common in many science libraries and collections. For high-use collections, it may be helpful to have the most popular journals, such as the journal titles listed in the appendix, available in print or electronic formats for patrons. Since most chemistry journals are available online and are the version of record, most print volumes can be transferred off-site if space is limited. It is recommended that print volumes not be withdrawn, especially ACS journals, since the license agreement provides access only: the library does not own the content if access is lost.

Identifying large monograph sets or annual book series, especially those that have ceased, is an easy way to quickly free up large amounts of shelf space by sending items off-site. Earlier editions of textbooks or other tertiary literature material can also be withdrawn or transferred off-site. Textbooks more than twenty years old can usually be withdrawn unless there is a historical need for them. Some selectors like to keep representative examples of earlier textbooks in the collection for historical purposes.

Conference proceedings more than twenty years old can be withdrawn, as they are not extensively used in chemistry. Exceptions to consider keeping include conferences of local and historical interest, or items where few libraries own the item. Older non-German language items can also usually be withdrawn as well, unless there is local or historical interest in the item. Older editions of reference materials can also be withdrawn or transferred off-site if space is limited.

PLANNING FOR FUTURE COLLECTIONS GROWTH

Planning for future growth is an ongoing activity. Publishing cycles can vary from year to year while collections budgets remain static; items are lost or go missing, or need to be weeded to make space for new titles, creating gaps in collections. Suggestions to help identify collection gaps and prepare for future budget years follow.

Chemistry books tend to remain in print for some time, usually two years or more for titles from major publishers. There is usually time to select a title later if funds are not immediately available. It is also helpful to check GOBI or other online approval databases to see the number of other libraries which have purchased the title. Checking popular title lists from publishers, approval vendors, and online book vendors is one way to ensure important titles are being selected for the collection. Many specialized titles, however, will be unlikely to show up on these lists and will need to be identified through other sources such as publishers' catalogs or online vendors.

Search the library and publisher catalogs for previously published major multivolume book and reference volumes when possible. These sets can get missed due to the high cost of materials and infrequent publication. Also consider allotting from 10 to 20 percent of the fund allocation to order older titles not in the collection. This will eliminate gaps in the historical collections while the titles are still available.

Consider ordering second copies of heavily used or titles that have been repaired or rebound. This will ensure enough copies of these titles are on hand for future library users. Likewise, extra copies of titles with little or no circulation can also be withdrawn.

Check library journal holdings against collections at peer institutions. Compiling lists of newer journal titles that faculty or researchers have requested also ensures that collections reflect changing research priorities and that important new titles get ordered. After new chemistry journals are introduced, there is often a time lag before faculty explore the area or consider the journal appropriate for the collection. Many professional society groups such as the Special Libraries Association are excellent sources for comparative serials cancellation lists.

Regular review of standing order titles in a library collection is essential to keep chemistry collections current. Many standing orders have irregular or infrequent publication cycles, which can result in volumes with high cost and low use. Consider canceling series that have not published additional volumes for more than two years. Standing orders that are comparable to the annual cost of a journal should also be critically examined, as the journal will likely be used more often.

Consider the case of access versus purchase of materials when selecting. Is current access to materials such as e-journals and e-books sufficient if a situation arises where ongoing access to the material cannot be maintained? Will archival access to titles be available indefinitely? Periodic review of coverage in online archives such as Portico are helpful in determining if publisher agreements are sufficient for accessing material in the long-term.

FINAL COMMENTS

Selecting in chemistry is a rewarding experience, although specialized terminology and tools and the emphasis on abstract ideas and terminology can make for a confusing environment. Keep in mind that many successful chemistry librarians were not trained as chemists and that a complete understanding of a subject is not necessary to successfully select materials. Having traditional reference skills and the enthusiasm to help patrons is as important as the subject knowledge.

The library collection is a growing, changing organism. Historical titles and materials can usually be obtained or acquired though gifts. Selecting books and journals in electronic and print formats is an intuitive process, so let your instincts guide you. Maintaining and building a balanced collection also requires some common sense. High-quality materials are usually identifiable by publisher reputation, appearance of the item, and positive reviews.

Finally, remember to enjoy the process of discovery and selection, and take the opportunity to learn new things about the collection, the subject of chemistry, and the creativity of its practitioners. Chemistry is a broad science and can enthrall everyone. Let it captivate you!

APPENDIX
CORE CHEMISTRY JOURNAL TITLES GROUPED BY SUBDISCIPLINE

A selection of highly cited and core journals in chemistry is organized by each major subdiscipline of chemistry. Titles are listed alphabetically by category and selected from the JCR Science Edition 2008 from Thompson Reuters, and sorted by Impact Factor for the chemistry subdivisions listed below.

Thompson Reuters ISI Web of Knowledge, *JCR-Web 4.5 Welcome*, http://admin-apps.isiknowledge.com/JCR/JCR?RQ=HOME (accessed March 22, 2012). (note: the JCR is a subscription database accessible for licensed users only).

The American Chemical Society (ACS) Committee on Professional Training (CPT) List of Recommended Journal List is consolidated into this list. The ACS CPT recommended titles are marked with an *. Titles selected as General content, Topical – Highly Recommended and Topical - Also Recommended are all included in the following list. The ACS CPT list was last revised in August 2008.

American Chemical Society Committee on Professional Training, *CPT-Recommended Journal List*, http://portal.acs.org/portal/PublicWebSite/about/governance/committees/training/acsapproved/CTP_006024 (accessed March 22, 2012).

TITLE CODE

- JCR journal titles are in *italics*.
- ACS CPT journal titles have asterisks (*).
- Titles on both lists are in *italics* and have an asterisk (*).

Multidisciplinary Chemistry

ACS Nano
**Accounts of Chemical Research*
**Advanced Materials*
**Angewandte Chemie International Edition*
**Bioconjugate Chemistry*
**Chemical Communications*
*The Chemical Educator
*Chemical Reviews
**Chemical Society Reviews*
**Chemistry - A European Journal*
Chemistry – An Asian Journal
*Chemistry Education: Research and Practice
*Chemistry Letters
*Combinatorial Chemistry and High Throughput Screening
Crystal Growth and Design
*Environmental Science and Technology
**Green Chemistry*
**Journal of the American Chemical Society (JACS)*
*Journal of Chemical Education
*Journal of Chemical Ecology
*Journal of Chemical Information and Modeling
**Journal of Chemical Theory and Computation*
*Journal of Combinatorial Chemistry
Journal of Controlled Release
Lab on a Chip
**Nano Letters*
*Nature

*New Journal of Chemistry
*Science
Pharmaceutical Research
*Proceedings of the National Academy of Science of the USA (PNAS)
Small
Topics in Current Chemistry

Analytical Chemistry

Analytical and Bioanalytical Chemistry
**Analytical Biochemistry*
**Analytical Chemistry*
Analytica Chimica Acta
**Analyst*
*Analytical and Bioanalytical Chemistry
Biosensors and Bioelectronics
Critical Reviews in Analytical Chemistry
*Electroanalysis
**Electrophoresis*
**Journal of the American Society for Mass Spectroscopy*
Journal of Analytical Atomic Spectrometry
Journal of Biomolecular Screening
**Journal of Chromatography* A
*Journal of Chromatography B
*Langmuir
Rapid Communications in Mass Spectroscopy
Sensors and Actuators B - Chemical
Talanta
TRAC – *Trends in Analytical Chemistry*

Biochemistry

*Advances in Protein Chemistry
**Analytical and Bioanalytical Chemistry*
*Biochemistry
*Biochemical Journal
**Bioconjugate Chemistry*
Bioinformatics
BMC Bioinformatics
*Bioorganic Chemistry

Briefings in Bioinformatics
*Chemical Biology (ACS)
*Critical Reviews in Biochemistry and Molecular Biology
Current Issues in Molecular Biology
*Current Opinion in Chemical Biology
Current Opinion in Biotechnology
Cytometry Part A
**Electrophoresis*
Expert Review of Proteomics
*FEBS Journal
*Journal of Biological Chemistry
*Journal of Biological Inorganic Chemistry
**Journal of Chromatography A*
*Journal of Chromatography B
*Journal of Medicinal Chemistry
*Journal of Molecular Biology
**Journal of Proteome Research*
Lab on a Chip
*Macromolecules
*Macromolecular Chemistry and Physics
Methods
Molecular & Cellular Proteomics
*Molecular Cell
Molecular Imaging
*Nature Chemical Biology
Nature Methods
Nature Protocols
*Nature Structural and Molecular Biology
*Organic and Biomolecular Chemistry
PLoS Computational Biology
Proteomics
*Supramolecular Chemistry
*Trends in Biochemical Science

Inorganic Chemistry

Advances in Inorganic Chemistry
Advances in Organomettallic Chemistry
Comments in Inorganic Chemistry

*Coordination Chemistry Reviews
Dalton Transactions
**European Journal of Inorganic Chemistry*
Gold Bulletin
**Inorganic Chemistry*
Inorganic Chemical Communications
Inorganica Chimica Acta
Journal of Biological Inorganic Chemistry
Journal of Inorganic Biochemistry
**Journal of Organomettallic Chemistry*
Journal of Solid State Chemistry
**Organometallics*
Polyhedron
Progress in Solid State Chemistry
Structure and Bonding
Tetrahedron-Asymmetry

Materials Science

ACS Nano
ACTA Materialia
**Advanced Functional Materials*
**Advanced Materials*
Annual Review of Materials Research
Carbon
**Chemistry of Materials*
Critical Reviews in Solid State and Materials Science
Crystal Growth & Design
International Journal of Plasticity
Journal of Materials Chemistry
Material Science Engineering R – Reports
MRS Bulletin
Materials Today
**Nano Letters*
Nature Materials
Nature Nanotechnology
Progress in Materials Science
Small
Soft Matter

Nanoscience and Nanotechnology

ACS Nano
Biomedical Microdevices
Biomicrofluidics
Biosensors & Bioelectronics
Current Nanoscience
Journal of Physical Chemistry C
Journal of Micromechanics and Microengineering
Journal of Nanoparticle Research
Lab on a Chip
Microfluidics and Nanofluidics
Microporous and Mesoporous Materials
Nanomedicine
**Nano Letters*
Nano Today
Nanotechnology
Nanotoxicology
Nature Nanotechnology
Plasmonics
Scripta Materialia
Small

Organic Chemistry

Advances in Carbohydrate Chemistry and Biochemistry
*Advances in Heterocyclic Chemistry
Advances in Organometallic Chemistry
*Advanced Synthesis & Catalysis
Aldrichimica acta
**Bioconjugate Chemistry*
**Biomacromolecules*
*Bioorganic Chemistry
Bioorganic & Medicinal Chemistry
*Current Organic Chemistry
**European Journal of Organic Chemistry*
Journal of Mass Spectrometry
*Journal of Medicinal Chemistry
**The Journal of Organic Chemistry*
*Journal of Organometallic Chemistry

Natural Product Reports
**Organic & Biomolecular Chemistry*
**Organic Letters*
**Organometallics*
**Synlett*
*Synthesis
**Tetrahedron*
Tetrahedron - Asymmetry
*Tetrahedron Letters

Physical Chemistry

Advances in Catalysis
Advances in Colloid and Interface Science
Advanced Functional Materials
**Advanced Materials*
Annual Reviews of Physical Chemistry
*Applied Catalysis A - General
Applied Catalysis B - Environmental
*Applied Spectroscopy
**Catalysis Reviews - Science and Engineering*
*Chemical Physics Letters
**Chemistry of Materials*
Current Opinion in Colloid & Interface Science
Faraday Discussions
International Reviews in Physical Chemistry
**Journal of Catalysis*
*The Journal of Chemical Physics
Journal of Materials Chemistry
Journal of Photochemistry and Photobiology C – Photochemistry Reviews
*Journal of Physical Chemistry A
*Journal of Physical Chemistry B
*Journal of Physical Chemistry C
Nature Materials
*Physical Chemistry Chemical Physics
Progress in Nuclear Magnetic Resonance Spectroscopy
Progress in Surface Science
Soft Matter

Structure and Bonding
Surface Science Reports

Polymer Chemistry

Advances in Polymer Science
**Biomacromolecules*
Carbohydrate Polymers
European Polymer Journal
*Journal of Applied Polymer Science
Journal of Biomaterials Science – Polymer Edition
Journal of Membrane Science
**Journal of Polymer Science Part A - Polymer Chemistry*
Macromolecular Bioscience
Macromolecular Chemistry and Physics
Macromolecular Rapid Communications
**Macromolecules*
Plasma Processes and Polymers
**Polymer*
Polymer Degradation and Stability
Polymer International
Polymer Review
Polymers for Advanced Technologies
Progress in Polymer Science
Reactive & Functional Polymers
Soft Matter

ABOUT THE AUTHOR

ELIZABETH BROWN is Scholarly Communications and Library Grants Officer and Chemistry, Applied Physics and Astronomy, Mathematical Sciences, Materials Science Librarian at Binghamton University Libraries in Binghamton, New York.

Brown holds a BA in Chemistry from the University of Virginia, an MS in Chemistry from the University of Pittsburgh and an MLIS in Librarianship from University of Texas-Austin.

CPSIA information can be obtained
at www.ICGtesting.com
Printed in the USA
JSHW081913140523
41673JS00002B/103

9 780838 985915